CAVETT ROBERT:
LEAVING A LASTING LEGACY

by Cavett Robert and Lee E. Robert

Creative Training Techniques International
7620 West 78th Street
Minneapolis, MN 55439-2518
(612) 829-1954

Publisher: Robert W. Pike
Editorial Coordinator: Barbara Petersen
Copyeditor: Pam Christian
Designer: Wendy Wormwood, Creative Renaissance

ISBN 1-56447-037-7
90000

9 781564 470379

■   ■   ■

To create a legacy is to plant a tree

under which you will never sit.

It is to look past your interests,

your hopes and your lifetime . . .

to put into motion changes

that will be an indelible inspiration

to those who follow.

Christopher J. Hegarty

■   ■   ■

FOREWORD

In life's adventure, the friends one makes bring the greatest and most lasting joy and fulfillment. My late husband, Norman Vincent Peale, had the privilege of knowing Cavett Robert, the subject of this book. The two often appeared on the same program at national business conventions.

Dr. Peale's friendship with Cavett was genuine. They delighted in sharing personal experiences and humorous events that occurred at speaking engagements, and in comparing notes on the possible impact each made with his public work.

I am proud that Lee Robert asked me to write the foreword for this wonderful book.

Ruth Stafford Peale

Ruth Stafford Peale
Chairman of the Board
Peale Center for Christian Living

ACKNOWLEDGMENTS

Bob Pike first met my father, Cavett Robert, in the 1980s. The two were waiting at Phoenix Sky Harbor Airport for a plane to Palm Desert, site of that year's National Speakers Association Convention. Accompanied by two of his young sons, Bob was impressed with how Cavett took time to talk to the boys, feel their muscles and make them feel important. He never forgot this gesture of kindness.

Perhaps it was this seed of admiration, planted years ago, that blossomed into Bob's offer to be our partner in making this "dream" book a reality. An inspiration and a dynamo, Bob has shown complete dedication to the publication of this book. It simply would not have happened without him. For this act of affection and generosity, we will be eternally grateful.

In addition to his personal efforts, Bob assembled a wonderful team to create this book, and we are grateful to each and every member. Glenna Salsbury, CSP, CPAE, allowed us to use her NSA presidency theme, "Leaving a Lasting Legacy," as the book's title. The National Speakers Association willingly made its collection of historical photos available. Barb Petersen put her organizational wizardry to work in coordinating the book's editing, production and printing. Pam Christian contributed her editorial expertise and personal enthusiasm for the project. Wendy Wormwood of Creative Renaissance developed the beautiful book design, format and layout.

I also would like to acknowledge my mother, Trudy Robert. Her help keeping Dad "honest" during the interviews, her tireless editing assistance and suggestions, and her unfailing encouragement and belief in this project made her our closest collaborator.

We extend a special thanks to George Morrisey, CSP, CPAE, and Rosita Perez, CPAE, for their help in gaining support for the publication of this book from NSA's CPAEs, past presidents and Cavett Award winners. We also gratefully acknowledge the help of those NSA members whose names are found on page 145.

And last, but far from least, a heartfelt thank you to the entire NSA "family" from the family of Cavett Robert.

Lee E. Robert
Phoenix Arizona
July, 1998

Contents

■   ■   ■

CONTENTS continued

■   ■   ■

An Interview
with
Cavett Robert

THE EARLY YEARS

TELL US ABOUT YOUR FIRST JOB.

I was born on November 14, 1907, near Starkville, Mississippi, on the Mississippi A&M (agricultural and mechanical) campus. My father was the highest-paid professor, next to the president, at Mississippi A&M College. He was dean of the Agricultural Department at that time, and he made $325 a month. We didn't have a lot of extra money to spend, so I always tried to make a little extra money.

I used to go down to the barbershop, and I was just old enough to go there by myself — 6 or 7. The barber was mighty good to me, and he gave me my first job. He used to give me 5 cents an hour on Saturdays to kill flies. I'd look forward to it. He would give me two hours of work, and that 10 cents was my spending money. Of course, you could go to a movie for 5 cents back in that day and time.

Another job I had was selling peanuts. There was a farmer on the edge of the campus who raised peanuts, and I had an arrangement with him where I could get them for a good price. I used to go to a grocery store up in Starkville—about a mile-and-a-half from Mississippi A&M College — and the grocer would give me some little bags . . . he wouldn't charge me for them. My mother would roast the peanuts and help me put them in the bags. Then, particularly over the weekends, I would walk over to campus and sell the peanuts for a nickel a bag. If I sold two or three bags, that was 15 or 20 cents, and that was an awful lot of money! I did that until I was 8 or 9, and then my real job came along.

Practically all of the professors at Mississippi A&M had a cow that would need to be milked. In the summers, most of the professors would go away to study. There was one big pasture on campus, and when the professors would go away, I had a contract with them to milk their cows. I would buy the hay . . . it cost very little . . . and I would milk their cows every morning and every afternoon. After I milked the cows, I'd take the milk and sell it to the campus dairy for so much a quart. They would have it churned and then they would sell the butter.

A big economic factor in the South was having cows, milking them, having the milk churned, getting the clabber and then getting the butter. Everyone did those things, and in the back of every home was a little garden. People would raise radishes, turnips, tomatoes and a few other things. That was all part of the way they would do it in the South. I did that in the summers from the time I was about 10 years old up until the time I went to high school. In the winter, I'd milk our own cow, and Pierre, my brother, would do it, too. We didn't get paid for that . . . it was one of our chores.

One other thing . . . we didn't make any money off them, but we had beehives — an apiary. My father was the only professor who had one. There were two kinds of bees: the old black bees and the fancy kind — the yellow bees. My father had plenty of room for them because we had the gardens. I was just crazy about the bees, and I wanted to raise them . . . they were so interesting.

My father taught me how you could go into a hive — we had one hive in particular — and smoke it. Whenever you'd get two queens in one hive, one would send the other away, and then some of the bees would swarm and settle somewhere else close by. We had a lot of empty hives around the garden, and I would go to the hive with the bees and smoke them very gently, and spray a little water on them so their wings would get wet and they couldn't fly away. Then I would take them and put them in an empty beehive. I would make sure to get the queen — there's always one queen — and I would try to get a pound of honey to put in the hive so they wouldn't leave. The bees would get used to you, and they were just as tame as could be. They would crawl all over you.

My father finally had 95 beehives, more than anyone in the county, and he was going to teach me to raise queen bees and advertise them, sell them and so forth. But we never got around to it. I always enjoyed the bees, though. Mr. Hummer, who lived in Macon, Mississippi, sold queen bees. The three little Hummer kids went to the school where I later taught at Prairie Point.

My father bought a little 40-acre farm when I was in grade school. He thought everybody ought to be reared on a farm. We raised cotton and corn and potatoes on that little farm, and we would work it even during the school year. To have your own corn and things like that was really fine. We even made our own syrup. We raised sugar cane, and you could have that squeezed and then heat it and prepare it. You could make sorghum and regular syrup . . . it's amazing how much of your own food you raised back in that day and time.

What was your childhood like in the summers?

Macon, Mississippi, which was 42 miles away, was where we all used to go in the summer for vacation. My mother's father was Emmett Cavett (we called him "Pappy"), and he was speaker of the house of the legislature in Jackson, Mississippi, but he lived in Macon. He had a farm — he raised cattle and cotton — and we always stayed there during the summer.

Now, Pappy's place was one of the greatest places! It was a typical farm . . . he had several hundred acres . . . and he would rent part of it out and get half the profits from the crops. I believe they called it "sharecropping."

Most of the farms had windmills, but we had a cistern. If you could go down deep enough, you could get a regular cistern. We had one of the best wells in the whole area. Just a little ways away was the Noxibee County Creek, and at a certain time of year when the water would get low, Pappy would rent a tank. The mules would pull it, and Pappy would fill that big ol' tank with water from the creek, then pour it into the cistern to fill it up. It would supplement the water in the well that way.

Having enough water was a real problem, and some people would have to beg for it. Some of the farmhouses farther away wouldn't give any water, so people would come over to our place. Pappy always said that everyone is entitled to water, so many of the black people would come and want to know if they could get water. Pappy was always giving plenty of water because we had a deep well.

Of course, we had our own orchard. We had our peaches and our oranges and our strawberries. And then there were the chickens. We had Rhode Island Reds and all different kinds of chickens. Everybody had to have eggs and chickens! Whenever we had guests coming . . . we had so many relatives in that area . . . Little Auntie and Uncle Allie, my mother's sister and her husband, would run out and catch a couple of chickens and they'd kill 'em and fry 'em. We had fried chicken and, of course, sausage. We had sweet potatoes and Irish potatoes, and we always had a lot of curd. We had biscuits and corn bread — corn bread was one of the main things.

■   ■   ■

During those summers at Pappy's, we'd attend the little Ex-Prairie Church, which was halfway between the school-house and Pappy's. The Ex-Prairie Church was a little Methodist church, and everybody knew everybody else. Every Sunday, we would go to church, and we would all take food and have "singing all day and dinner on the ground." The day was spent going to church, picnicking, singing and visiting with friends.

WHAT KIND OF CLOTHING DID YOU WEAR GROWING UP?

When I was a little boy growing up, my family was fairly big, so we thought in terms of inheriting the clothes of your older brother. You would have a "Sunday go to meeting" outfit and an everyday outfit. You didn't change as often back then as you do now. The thing that I looked forward to so much, and all little kids did, was that some-day I'd get to wear long pants. A lot of the boys growing up wore shorts and also what we called "knickers." These were pants that came just below your knee, and then you would wear black stockings. When you got close to your teens, you looked forward to wearing long pants, just like the girls would look forward to the time when they could get their ears pierced.

We would go down to Starkville, and they always had the long pants hanging on a rack outside of the shop. My first pair of long pants I got from my older brother, Pierre, when he got too big for them. I inherited them, and I remember they were fancy and made out of corduroy.

WHAT WERE SOME OF THE TRADITIONS YOU HAD IN THE SOUTH?

So many people lived in isolated areas — in small towns and rural communities. There were certain family tradi-tions that you carried on — for instance, everybody went to church. You had Sunday school, and everybody knew everybody else. A tradition on Friday nights was The Joy Club, where all the kids got together and played games. We didn't have TV or radio, so the only entertainment we had was to get together and entertain ourselves. We'd get together over at someone's house who had children — it rotated from week to week — and we'd play games like hide and seek, drop the handkerchief and pin the tail on the donkey.

At Christmas, we had the tradition of getting the Christmas tree . . . they didn't sell them back then like they do now. I remember Mr. Schmell had a lot of young pines on his property, and he would make it possible for us to come pick one of the trees about a month before Christmas, and that would be our tree. He made sure that no one else would get your tree.

We would get the tree a couple of weeks before Christmas, and we would decorate it and put the presents under it. At noon on Christmas Eve day was when the holiday officially started. On Christmas Eve, we lit the candles. We would have a big banquet, and in our family, it was a tradition to have pilau. It was made with guinea hen and rice and was heavily peppered. We cooked it in the fireplace, and we would eat it sitting around a table next to the fire, with the Christmas tree looking so beautiful. This was not where we usually ate, but it was special for Christmas Eve, because this was where we hung the stockings.

After the banquet, we hung the stockings over the fireplace. We were all a little jealous of each other and would make sure no one hung their stocking too close to the other. We wrote a note to Santa Claus and left pilau and molasses pie for him. Then we blew out the candles and went to bed. There was always the danger of a fire, so we never left the candles burning. Then Santa Claus would come and put his presents under the tree, and the next morning, Mother and Dad would light the candles again.

On Christmas day, early in the morning — about 4 or 5 a.m. — the servants from all over the area would wake us up by saying, "Christmas gift! Christmas gift!" Then, we would say to our sisters and brothers and anyone you'd meet with during the day, "Christmas gift!" If you said it first, then the other person owed you a present! Of course,

3

you might not get a present, but it was a fun game. About 1 p.m., we would have a special Christmas dinner with turkey and curd and a lot of things.

Birthdays were another big tradition, and you made a big to-do over someone's birthday. You always had a birthday party. People would bring presents — not expensive things, a bar of candy or something. We would play games, and at school, they would write "Happy Birthday" on the chalkboard.

In that day and time in the South, we looked for opportunities to celebrate, because we didn't have a lot of the other forms of entertainment available today. You could see a moving picture only about once a week, and they were "silent films." When you were too young to read, you'd sit there and your mother would read the dialogue to you.

When "Maa Maa" — my grandmother on my mother's side — became too blind to see very well, Mother would read to her at the movies and whisper in her ear. People would move away from us because it would interfere with them. People around us would hiss, "Not so loud . . . not so loud!" Dad used to give Mother hell for it, and she would say, "It's more important to me that my mother hears the movie." He would say, "Yes, but you're annoying those people," and she would answer, "Well, that's just too bad . . . I'm going to do it anyway."

We had a newsreel to start with, and then the movie. About halfway through, we had a 10-minute intermission, and there was a cartoon. There were a lot of serials back then, like *The Lone Ranger*. They would stop the movie at a cliff-hanging moment, and you had to come back the next week to see what happened. Looking back on them now, they were so jerky and jumpy . . . the technology wasn't at all sophisticated. But at that time, I just thought they were wonderful.

4

In that day and time, teachers were looked up to more than they are today. My teachers, before we went into higher education, were really considered the acme . . . the ultimate. You looked up to them, and you depended on them so much. It was necessary that you had their approval, because — outside of your parents and maybe your relatives — you just didn't have a lot of things flowing your way. It was very important that they provide you with things.

I got a dime a week allowance, and I'd take care of it and carry it with me. I had a safety pin to close my pocket so I wouldn't lose it. Popcorn, peanuts, candy and movies were what I would spend it on. On my birthday, I'd get a quarter, and I'd buy string to sail my kite.

I don't know that you would call them a tradition, but outhouses were a way of life in the summer at Pappy's. During the year, when we lived at Mississippi A&M, we had inside plumbing. But on the farms, no one had inside plumbing, so when we went to Pappy's, we used the outhouses.

There was an outhouse for the men, which was down in the orchard, and if all seats were being used, you could go down to the barn. The women's outhouse was right outside the main house, in back of the chicken house. The women had a four-hole outhouse, and the men had three holes. After a meal, everyone would go down there with the Sears-Roebuck catalogue as toilet paper, and the newspaper. It was a very sociable event, and the men and women would go out together to their separate outhouses.

Maa Maa was the only one who had a little glass jar in her room — called a "slop jar" — that the servants would take out to the orchard every day and dump. The only way we would get to use a slop jar would be maybe if we were very ill. Otherwise, the rest of us always used the outhouses. Maa Maa also had real toilet paper.

There were lots of traditions in the South. For those attending college, there was the tradition of pledging for a fraternity or sorority. If a boy got to the point with a girl where she was his sweetheart, he would give her his pledge

■   ■   ■

pin. That was pretty serious, just before an engagement and a diamond ring! That meant she was your sweetheart, and she wasn't supposed to date anyone else.

There was also the tradition of eating watermelon in the summer when I was growing up. We had 19 grandchildren at Pappy and Maa Maa's, so they always had to cut two watermelons and divide them around. I remember that Maa Maa always got the heart of the watermelon, and the kids always got the rind with a little fruit on it. Pappy used to cut a big piece out of the middle and eat it, saying he was just "testing it" to make sure it was good. We also had cantaloupe for anyone who didn't want watermelon. There were a couple of the relatives that didn't like watermelon, and we just thought that was the strangest thing.

There was the tradition in the community that if anyone got married, the girl would have a shower. The more showers you had, the more prominent you were in the community. My aunt and uncle, the Swans, would put on a shower and invite everyone in the county. Everybody was supposed to bring a present, and it was amazing the things they would bring — ham, canned goods, kitchen utensils, plates, a shawl, a hat . . . things you could use. The shower hosts didn't specify what to bring, like they do today.

People were supposed to come the day before the shower, anytime before noon, to bring their presents. Many would call ahead of time and ask, "Does the couple have this?" or "Do they have that?" They would try so hard not to have duplications in presents. People would save things in their homes, saying, "I'm saving this for a shower someday."

The maid of honor — usually, you had a family member or your closest friend — was almost as important as the bride. It was considered a great honor to be asked to be a bridesmaid. When Sis was picked, she considered it one of the greatest honors of her whole life. There would be three or four bridesmaids per wedding.

The wedding was really put on for the community, and the family would always have a rehearsal that the relatives would attend. The Swans had their whole front yard decorated . . . it was an acre or so. In the back, they served punch and food. They had a beautiful gazebo for the ceremony to take place in. The gazebo had a piano that had been moved to one side.

The wedding was really a shindig! The bride and bridesmaids were hidden behind the bushes. The music started, and the preacher came out and would read from the Bible. Then, the "Wedding March" began playing, and the bridesmaids came out, joined by the groom and the groomsmen . . . they would always try to have the same number of groomsmen and bridesmaids. Then came the little flower girl and the ring bearer and finally, the bride, led by her father, who'd give her away. The bride and groom would say their vows, and the rings would be exchanged, much like today.

The reception was held after the wedding, and then the honeymoon would start after the reception, and the guests would usually go home. There isn't so much difference today compared to what we did back then, but there was so little entertainment then that a wedding was considered the highlight of the whole year.

Getting the mail was also a big deal, a daily ritual, when we would stay out at Pappy's farm. Pappy lived about two-and-a-half or three miles from Macon, Mississippi. There was a gravel road for about a mile or so from town, and then there was a dirt road from there on. The home was about 150 or 200 yards from the dirt road. We could see practically all the way down to the big gravel road.

At certain times, Mr. Durrow, the mailman, would deliver the mail in his big Ford car. But when the weather was bad, he would deliver it in his horse-drawn buggy. It was usually about 8 o'clock in the morning when he would deliver it, and my grandfather would sit there on the front porch and look for him. When we were visiting in the summer, Joe and Pierre and I would sit out there on the porch and wait with Pappy, and when we'd see Mr. Durrow, we'd shout, "Pappy . . . here comes Mr. Durrow!" That was the big event every day except Sunday. The Sunday paper would come on Monday.

Pappy would let us walk down the hill a little bit in the mud to pick up the mail and bring it back to him. Mr. Durrow would always take such pride in giving us the mail and saying, "How's Mr. Cavett?" The thing that my grandfather was more anxious to get than anything else was *The Commercial Appeal,* a Memphis paper — that was the big paper. Of course, there was a local paper from Macon, Mississippi, but *The Commercial Appeal* was akin to *The New York Times* or *The Washington Post.* Occasionally, it wouldn't come, so Pappy would always holler when we brought the mail back up to him, "Did *The Commercial Appeal* come with it?"

When I lived on the Mississippi A&M campus, we had to walk across campus about a mile from where we lived to get the mail. Billie Hayes, a track coach at the college, had the post boxes in his store. To this day, I can practically remember the combination to our box. We used to get the mail there at about 4 in the afternoon.

TELL US ABOUT THE KITES YOU FLEW AS A BOY.

There were two kinds of kites — one was the regular kite, and then later on, if you got where you were very skillful, you made a box kite. I remember the Mitchell brothers used to bring their box kite down to the school, and during the recess, they would fly it. Even the teachers would come out to see it, and the Mitchell brothers would explain how they made it. If ever you made a box kite that would fly, that was really impressive.

You had to be very careful with any kind of kite, because if you made it and the first time you tried to fly it, it dove down, it would break. But if you had one that would stay in the air, that was really something. You'd have the neighbors come around to see it. They'd ask, "How long did it stay up?" And you'd say, "All day, if we wanted it to!" We'd brag about it!

When flying kites, you'd borrow people's string and you'd lend string. String cost about 10 cents to have enough to get your kite about twice the height of the trees. You'd save the string that came tied around packages and tie it to your ball of string to lengthen it. On a birthday, if you wanted to give something very special, you'd give kite string.

During winter, you'd put the kites in the attic and wait until spring came. If the wind came up, it was a good kite day. You had to kind of watch out, because sometimes the reason the wind came up was because it was going to rain, and if you got rain on your kite, it would ruin it. We'd say, "Dad, do you think I could sail my kite today?" He'd say, "No, I don't think so . . . the wind's so strong." But I'd say, "Oh, no . . . I'll take it down to the field." And if it dove down and broke, you lost your kite, because you couldn't fix them after that . . . they wouldn't fly. So, you really had to preserve those kites.

EDUCATION AND MENTORS

WHAT WAS YOUR SCHOOLING LIKE?

Education was very important in my family. My schooling started with grade school at Mississippi A&M College, and Miss Foster taught the grammar school. Miss Foster was a very dear woman and a good psychologist, and her husband was Mr. Monosmith, who had the greenhouse. I loved Miss Foster.

They finally closed down that little school, and all of us had to go to Starkville, which was about two-and-a-half or three miles from Mississippi A&M. I started high school there, and they had different teachers for different subjects. That's when I really developed an inferiority complex.

It was there that I entered my first speech contest, and I forgot my speech. My brothers were both excellent speakers, and I felt so much pressure to measure up to them that I panicked. "On the return of the soldier to his native land, what did he do, this hero in gray with a heart of gold . . . ," I started, then my mind went blank. I said again, ". . . what did he do, this hero in gray with a heart of gold . . . ," but the words still wouldn't come to me. After the third round of ". . . what did he do, this hero in gray with a heart of gold . . . ," a kid in the front row said, "I'll bite . . . what did he do?" I ran from the stage. That was my junior year in high school, and I was so humiliated that I wouldn't go back to school, and Mother had to tutor me for the rest of the year.

I had such terrible malaria fever during that time. Finally, the doctor told me that I should leave Mississippi. So I went up to Greenville, South Carolina, where my sister's husband, Frank P. Gaines (we called him "Brother"), was teaching English at Furman University. I lived with Sis and Brother and went to high school at Greenville High for my senior year, which I enjoyed.

During the school year, I lived with Sis and Brother, but during the summer when they went away (Brother was working on his Ph.D.), I had to make arrangements for myself. I got a job at Furman waiting on tables in the summer in order to get my meals free. I also got my room free for making up a number of the rooms. I had a contract with the cleaning people to pick up the clothes, and they would give me a small percentage.

I entered the Declamation Contest — a speaking contest there at Greenville High School — and I won it for the boys. A preacher's daughter won it for the girls. The event was called the Dialect Literary Society in Mississippi, and they called it the Declamation Contest there in Greenville. I worked so hard on that speech, and I got Brother to help me with it. I would write it out, and he would make suggestions on how we could change it. Brother helped me a lot, and I couldn't have done it without him.

After I graduated from Greenville High School and before I entered Furman as a college freshman, I was a lifesaver for the Furman University pool, and that gave me $15 a month. While I was a lifesaver, I met Trudy, my future wife. This was even before I was a student under her father at Furman. A lot of the professors' little sons and daughters would go swimming there at the Furman University pool. Trudy was about 12 years old, and I was about 17. She pushed me into the pool to get my attention!

I went to Furman for one year and six months. One prominent person I went to school with was Herman Lay, who would eventually become head of Frito-Lay. I had a lot of stomach trouble at the time, and the doctors said that I had anemia. Because of this, I didn't finish my second year at Furman and went out to stay with Mother and Dad, who were living at Pappy's place at the time. Dad was retired from teaching then and selling insurance.

I went to Milsaps College in Jackson, Mississippi, for three months during the summer. I got all the units I had failed to get at Furman, so I had enough that I could enter the University of Mississippi. I got the money to go to the University of Mississippi, a state school, through a scholarship. It was $125 for the year. Because I got the scholarship, school didn't cost me anything . . . and Mother let me have a little money she'd saved to live on, too.

"Ol' Miss" was the most glamorous school in the state. I filed my application and was approved, and during the summer, a bunch of the fraternities "rushed" me. If you wanted to join them and they wanted to accept you, that was fine. Several of the K A's gave me the rush, but there were four or five Sigma Chi's from Macon, Mississippi, so I wanted to join them.

If you joined a fraternity, you would pledge for the first half of the year. There were about 10 of us at the Sigma Chi house. A very nice lady there charged us about $10 a month. I met the two Pleasant brothers there, Jim and Pep Pleasant, and Charlie Ferris. Our house was just at the edge of the campus, and we had a lot of fun there.

It was the first time I'd ever been to a coed school. We had Sigma Chi meetings once a week. The Sigma Chi's and a sorority at the school would go to party after party together, and I was really very sensitive to sitting in classes where there were women. We'd all wait to see who would get to sit at the back of the class, because we were all very timid. But I enjoyed it very much.

I was the fraternity's rush captain one year, and we would look the young guys over. The Sigma Chi members in other geographic areas would write to us and tell us who were the hot prospects. We'd invite the kids to dinner, and we'd have rush parties. We'd all get together and ask the new kids to stand up and tell about their background.

I lived in the Sigma Chi house and went to Ol' Miss for my last two years of college. I earned a B.A. and a B.S. because I had more units than I needed. They asked me which I wanted — a B.A. or a B.S.? — and I believe I have "B.A." on my diploma from the University of Mississippi.

YOU WERE NAMED AFTER GENERAL HENRY CAVETT ROBERT, YOUR GREAT UNCLE AND AUTHOR OF ROBERT'S RULES OF ORDER. WHY DID YOU CHANGE YOUR NAME?

I had a scholarship to one of the colleges I went to. They had to have my legal name, and I thought that would be a good time to shorten it. I found that people were always calling me "Hank," and I didn't like it.

It's very simple to change a name. A lot of people change their names, for a variety of reasons. At the time I changed mine, I hadn't gotten into law yet. I didn't realize there was a certain prestige to being named after General Henry Robert . . . or else maybe I wouldn't have had it changed!

WHO WERE SOME OF YOUR MENTORS EARLY IN LIFE?

I had such wonderful examples set for me early in life. I just worshiped my grandfather, Emmett Duvergne Cavett, whom we called Pappy. And I practically worshiped my brother-in-law, Francis Pendleton Gaines, whom we called

Brother. I saw these people accomplish so much. Furthermore, I was so impressed by my two brothers' successes. I wanted success so strongly, I almost had an insane ambition . . . I wanted to follow in their footsteps. Len King, a cousin of mine, was a wonderful person . . . he was a professor out there at Mississippi A&M.

I believe that the most powerful influence you can have as you go along is wanting to imitate people you admire. I was fortunate enough to be surrounded by people that I admired very much. I don't think there was anybody who was ever exposed to more people he admired than I was, and I was inspired to imitate them. I would imitate certain people, and I was fortunate enough to have them encourage me and tell me I could do it, and they'd make me believe it. I was exposed to the fact that the most powerful force in the world is knowing someone believes in you, and you don't want to disappoint them.

Miss Foster

The grammar school at Mississippi A&M was one room in the Textile Mill Building, and Miss Foster ran the school. Miss Foster was a very prim and proper lady, with her hair pulled up tight in a bun. She taught that first year, and toward the end of the year, I got to where I was so in love with her . . . she was just like a mother to me . . . that I would stay after school if she would let me.

I started out with Miss Foster in the first grade, and when the second grade came along, she would say, "You are just as smart as your brothers, but in a different way!" Thank goodness she never told me in what way, because I had a hard time learning my multiplication tables, and I would try to give any little verse and get mixed up. But she would never let me get discouraged, and she would always brag on me.

I remember Mr. Monosmith, who ran the greenhouse for the college, had a son who also went to grammar school there. Mr. Monosmith would come to the school in the afternoons, and we would all sit together. It was announced that Miss Foster was going to marry Mr. Monosmith, and she made us all feel so good, like it was the merging of a family.

9

I had a lot of trouble, because my folks were not well off financially, and I had to miss school one time because I didn't have shoes to wear. I remember I went to school once, and my feet were just blue they were so cold. Miss Foster sent me home to get some shoes. Mother and I went downtown to get some shoes, and she asked the store clerk if we could charge them. We were turned down, so I couldn't take the shoes. Miss Foster was very understanding about it.

I used to tell Miss Foster about my brothers, Joe and Pierre. They went to another school, and I had such an inferiority complex. That was when she would build me up, and it was just what I needed at that time. She was someone outside the family that recognized me and helped to build my confidence. That kind of encouragement, I needed so much at that time in my life. I hope Miss Foster has a special place in heaven, because she knew what my problem was and really helped try to solve it.

Coach Hayes

Billie Hayes — a track coach at Mississippi A&M who coached three people for the Olympics later on — took an interest in me and let me watch some of the great college track men, although I was only in grammar school and high school. He wasn't paid enough to live on, so he had a little store there on the campus called The Shack, where he sold books and candy. I'd go in there to buy a candy bar occasionally and see him. Coach Hayes took an interest in me . . . I was the kid of one of the professors . . . and he let me come down and jog with him. I had a great ambition to be an athlete.

When I was 9 or 10 years old, we lived in a house on the campus of Mississippi A&M, and right at the end of our backyard was the big cinder racetrack where all the athletes used to train. One day, I wandered down there, and I saw Coach Hayes. I'd ask him about some of the athletes, and I would sit with him . . . I admired him so. Coach Hayes would tell me about Murph and Catchell and Spencer — he had three people on the Olympic team at one time. These people would run 100 yards and Coach Hayes would time them, and it was so exciting when they'd gain an eighth of a second! Most of the other tracks were of a harder substance, but the cinder track we had was harder to run on. The effect was like training horses in water — when the runners ran on other tracks, they made better time because it was easier.

I just worshiped Coach Hayes, and he knew it. One day, he said to me, "Why don't you trot around with the athletes? They aren't really going to run, they're just exercising for a few laps." He gave me a pair of track shoes that I treasured more than anything I had in life. I kept those shoes up until the time I got into college. They got to the point where I'd outgrown them, but I still treasured them and displayed them on the wall.

WHO WAS THE GREATEST MENTOR IN YOUR ADULT LIFE?

Dr. Norman Vincent Peale was probably the man I admired most in my life and who had the greatest overall influence on my life.

When I was going to Washington and Lee University for three years, studying law, I lived in the Lee Home, which was the university president's home. At the end of the Civil War, Robert E. Lee had become president there, and they changed the name from Washington College to Washington and Lee University. My brother-in-law, Frank Gaines, was president at the time I attended Washington and Lee. Dr. Peale had a son who went to school there, too, and when Dr. Peale would come and visit his son, Dr. Gaines would have him stay in the Lee Home . . . it had about seven bedrooms. Because I lived there at the time, I got to know Dr. Peale very well. He was wonderful to me and gave me so much advice, and he appreciated so much my brother-in-law having him there.

When I went to New York to practice law, Dr. Peale took me under his wing, and I went to his church, The Marble Collegiate Church. He arranged for me at times to teach at his Sunday school, particularly with the kids. He would encourage me and even invited me to his family's home several times. I used to go to his classes, and I almost memorized his book, *The Power of Positive Thinking*.

I asked Dr. Peale to speak at a few meetings I was interested in — Toastmasters and so forth — and he was gracious and would do it. Then, of course, when I was starting the National Speakers Association, I used to go and discuss it with him. He would always say, "Don't give up on it. The NSA might fail a couple more times . . . it's been tried before." But then he would make the statement, "There's nothing that can't be accomplished when the right people are swept up in a worthy cause, divorced from who gets credit for what." He said, "If you will stay with it, I guarantee I will help you. And if you call on me sometime, I'll come and speak for you." He did indeed come to NSA's rescue about a year later at our annual meeting in New Orleans. We picked up about 300 new members because of his participation, and that was our big start.

Dr. Bob Schuller has also had a big effect on my life. I met him through a friend of mine, Danny Cox, who was on the NSA's board of directors. Danny arranged for Dr. Schuller to have me on the program at The Crystal Cathedral Church. The husband of Merlyn Cundiff, my associate at the time, was at the church, and he was dying of cancer. I spoke about 30 minutes, then Dr. Schuller asked, "Is there anyone you think we ought to say a prayer for?" I said, "My associate's husband is dying of cancer, and he is in the audience. Let's pray for him." Dr. Schuller asked Merlyn's husband to stand up, and he said a prayer for him.

Dr. Schuller asked me to speak two or three times for different groups at the church, and twice he asked me to go to Jerusalem. The first time I went, I got to know the attendants, and Dr. Schuller was so wonderful to me. The second time, Dr. Schuller's son — who was the head of the trip — developed a bad case of the flu and couldn't speak. Dr. Schuller asked me if I could take over. For nine days, I held the evening prayer meeting, and Dr. Schuller was so grateful for that.

To raise money for building the Crystal Cathedral, Dr. Schuller "sold" windows and pews . . . buyers could dedicate them to whomever they chose. I "bought" a window for my mother and a window for her sister and my favorite aunt, Allie Swan (Little Auntie). Dr. Schuller had to raise more money than he thought and decided to sell the other side of the windows, too. I was so afraid that a criminal would get on the other side of those precious windows that I decided to buy the other side, too!

One of the greatest business leaders I observed in my life was the president of the Chemical Bank and Trust Company. His name was Percy H. Johnston Jr., and he was my friend, Duke Johnston's, father. He also became president of the American Association of Bankers and built his bank up to be one of the biggest in the country.

Percy Johnston Jr., permitted me to sit in on some of the meetings he held, and I remember he said the foremost quality of a good banker was the ability to make every person feel important and realize that they played a vital role in the future of banking. He wasn't just talking to vice presidents and managers; he made every person . . . the people out on the floor, every employee . . . feel like they were an integral part of the success of the bank. This great man made people realize they could play a part and make a difference, that they were not lost in the maze of this big corporation. I've tried to follow his example in business.

12

THE ROBERT FAMILY TREE

TELL US ABOUT THE FAMILY YOU GREW UP IN.

Frank Gaines ("Brother")

Dr. Gaines, my brother-in-law, was really an inspiration to our whole family, until later on, when he became very ill. For the first few years I knew him, he was the greatest inspiration to me. He became a professor at Mississippi A&M College. My mother and father hired him to tutor my sister, Sadie Duvergne. A lot of people back then had teachers who were mentors, and Dr. Gaines lived in our home. That's when he and Sadie fell in love. They were in love for a couple of years, and then they were married. Sadie was just 18. While Coach Billie Hayes was kind of a mentor to me physically, Dr. Gaines was my mentor spiritually and mentally. He taught Sunday school at the First Baptist Church, and he brought so much literature into his talks.

People were married so much earlier back then. My mother married when she was 17 or 18, and my grandmother married when she was 16. Back in that day and time, the parents in most cases selected who you were going to marry. Everyone lived so far apart, and they didn't have a lot of the opportunities that people have today to meet people.

The wedding of my sister and Dr. Gaines really was a social event. They had a big wedding, and everybody turned out — the whole college turned out. The wedding really went down in history there. I'll never forget how they had the George Rifle and the Lee Guards, two fraternities there, wearing their uniforms and putting their rifles up into an arch. Dr. Gaines and Sadie Duvergne walked under the arch while Dr. Leak had his orchestra play.

Leonard King, who had roomed with Dr. Gaines in college, came in as a professor at Mississippi A&M and married my cousin, Dora Evelyn Connor, who was very beautiful. Dr. Gaines and Sadie Duvergne's wedding had set a pattern. Dora Evelyn and Leonard King were married the same way, although they didn't have quite the big to-do that Brother and Sis had. The two couples were friends throughout their lives.

I admired Dr. Gaines so much while he lived in our home, and he took such an interest in me. I was about 12 years old, Sis was about 18 and Dr. Gaines was about 22 or 23. He was kind of a teacher to me, and he would brag on me and ask me about my schoolwork.

If I made B's or A's, I'd come in and tell him about it, and he would want to know all the details. He would come down and talk to our grammar school . . . all the professors did that. He seemed to know how to interest young people and was an excellent speaker.

I looked up to Dr. Gaines because he gave such a wonderful spiritual message when he talked to our grammar school and high school. He used to encourage me, because I wanted to be able to speak like my brothers, Joe and Pierre, who were in the Dialect Literary Society. Both of them had won contests and were so accomplished in this way.

'Little Auntie'

"Little Auntie," as we called my mother's sister, was quite a spiritual teacher to me, too. She was married to Allie Swan, who was a big farmer in Starkville and was on the board of supervisors of the county. The farmers back then had a couple of ways of hiring help. One of the ways was that they would pay workers a salary, and the other was where the farmers would rent land out and get a percentage of the profits from the sale of the harvest — I believe they called it "sharecropping."

Uncle Allie had a little store in Starkville, primarily food — potatoes, corn and some staples like that — and a few clothes. He would advance people things that they needed, and then they would pay him twice a year when the crops came in. It was a whole different way of living, because people didn't have a lot of money until the crops came in.

People would come in from Jackson and Columbus with their trucks and bring their crops to sell to Uncle Allie. Then the wholesalers would come in and buy the produce and pay Uncle Allie, and then he would go back to the farmers and settle with them.

You didn't have much social life back then. I would ride a horse to get to The Joy Club, or sometimes I would ride my horse before dark to Mr. Bogus's house, and he would take us and his two kids in a wagon. The Joy Club was where we would meet people socially. First, you'd go in and meet everybody . . . there was always a lady who would be in charge of it and see that even the timid ones would talk to people. Then we would sing songs and play games like ring-around-the-rosey. The best thing was hide-and-seek, because you might get a chance to kiss someone behind a bush. I can't remember that I ever actually did it, but I always wanted to. My brother Pierre and Matty Bell did, though, and if they didn't come back in a hurry, you'd know they were necking. The Joy Club and the church were where you'd get to see everybody and socialize.

Little Auntie was on the board of supervisors of the school, and she knew all the parents. She had a lot of children — Porter and Little Allie and Louise and Hallie Lee and Bess . . . she had seven children in all — so naturally, she would promote The Joy Club. She would always say, "You're going to come to The Joy Club, aren't you? You be sure to be there! If you can't get there, I'll make sure to have someone pick you up." We'd have a big crowd of 30 to 35 children there.

Little Auntie taught Sunday school and played the organ at the little Ex-Prairie Church down where the Tom Bigby and Buddy Hatchie rivers came together. I started going to that church where she taught Sunday school, and she was so nice to me. She told me that I could come and visit her whenever my mother went away on a trip. My mother was away so much during that time visiting Brother and Sis. When I was 16 to 19, I had malaria fever. The mosquitoes were so bad that you always had to sleep under a mosquito net. I didn't respond to the quinine they treated you with back then. I would have fever, and Little Auntie would say, "Now, if your mother is away and you ever get sick, stop by here and I'll take care of you." She bought me a dog, and I named it Sport.

Little Auntie always welcomed me into her home. When I got sick, I used to go by there, and she would nurse me and be sweet to me and tell me that the parents thought I was doing a great job teaching their kids. She would talk religion to me. It was at a time when I was always so afraid that I was going to go to hell. She would talk about God as a loving spirit . . . she would love me into the church rather than scare me into it.

Mother (Hallie Cavett Robert)

After the war, my mother taught the war students. That was about 1918, I believe, and I was about 11 years old. My mother was the dean for these war students. When they needed about three more teachers, my mother got jobs for Rosa and Sally Span, her sister's oldest daughters, and Dora Evelyn, my cousin . . . the one who eventually married Len King.

I just worshiped my mother. She used to correct me about certain things, and she'd say, "Now, if you love me, you won't ever do that again." And if ever I would do anything wrong, she would say, "This makes me feel that you don't love me, because if you did, you would follow what I tell you to do. You knew that would hurt me and was not the right thing to do." That would upset me more than anything. I would say, " 'Scuse me, Momma . . . please will you 'scuse me?"

I thought that if Mother excused me about anything, then that was kind of like the Pope giving forgiveness . . . everything would be bright after that. Momma would say, "I'll excuse you this time if you promise me you'll never do that again." I would say, "Momma, I promise I'll never do it again . . . I'll neeeeever do it again!" She'd say, "OK, kiss me now . . . you're excused." It was like being given absolution of a sin! I would say, "Oh, thank you, Momma, thank you!" I would just feel so happy!

I was the baby of the family, and I had an inferiority complex because Joe and Pierre and Sis were just so brilliant. In that day and time, being the oldest gave you priority. If there were only three candy bars and there were four of us, well, it was the youngest who wouldn't get one. There was just something about being older that had the advantage — there was a pecking order. If someone was going to town and there were four of us and only room for three in the car, then the oldest ones got to go and the youngest had to stay home. Sometimes, it felt like I was a second-class citizen because I was the youngest. Age was a real advantage.

My mother always wanted to see that I was looked after, but she liked to go visit Pappy and go visit with Sis and Brother in South Carolina. If there wasn't enough money for all of us to go, I would have to stay home with Dad. He meant well, but he was not a very warm person. I would sometimes want to come and cuddle with Mom and Dad when I was little, and he wouldn't want me there and would tell me to go back to bed. My mother would come and cuddle me and kiss me goodnight. There was an almost religious feeling between my mother and me.

Even now, Hal . . . that was my mother's nickname . . . is like a guardian angel to me. I can hear her voice at times saying, "Don't worry, Cavee . . . don't worry." She would call me her "little Cavee." She would tell me stories, and if I wanted a story told to me before I went to bed, I would kneel down at her feet and put my head in her lap and say my prayers. She would say, "Now I'm going to tell you a story," and she would change her voice and make it so dramatic. She would tell me the story of Ol' Gooley Young and sing the song, "Gooley Young-Young-Young-Young, Gooley Young-Young-Young-Young . . . so light and so gay, so sing Gooley Young." She told me The Snake Tale, too. Both of these were her own creations, but she would also tell me Grimms' fairy tales. She could tell a story in a way to make it so exciting! I remember Jack, the Giant Killer!

Was your mother the disciplinarian in your family?

Yes, but she would always have a way of talking to me: "If you love me, I know you'll do it." My dad would use the strap, but my mother would have a way of loving me into doing the right thing.

15

So your mom was a loving disciplinarian, but she had definite rules about things?

She did. The main thing was that she wanted you to live by certain rules. You were supposed to go to bed by a certain time, you were supposed to study, and you couldn't use foul language. When my mother was teaching and making money, she had a certain budget, and she would live by it. She would have so much for the church, and she had a servant who looked after her named Mandy, who had a salary. She also had two other servants — Charlie Tabb and his wife, Annie — who loved Mother and looked after her. Whenever we would go down to Macon to visit Pappy, both of them would come, and Charlie would cut the grass and Annie would clean the house. Annie would come practically every day and cook for us, too.

How did your mother feel about religion?

I remember so well that we used to have revival meetings in this big hall, and there was a traveling evangelist who would come there every year. One time, my friends Gene and Chess Chadwick and one or two others and I went to the meeting and sat in the first row. The evangelist got up there and said, "If you do not give your soul to Christ, you will die in hell . . . in hell, in hell! Be lost . . . lost! Gone to hell!" He ranted for an hour or two.

I remember one night, he ranted forth and said, "If you don't want to burn in hell, eternal hell, then come up and shake hands and demonstrate to the world that you have given your soul to Jesus." Then he gave us an opportunity to come up and shake hands. We went back and forth trying to decide, and we decided we were going to do it. So, we went up and shook hands with him. Seemed like a small price to pay to avoid burning in hell for all eternity! The evangelist said, "God bless you, and now you will go to heaven."

We were really happy about our experience, and when I got home, I told my mother and dad. I told them we had gone up there and shaken hands with the man and given our soul to Jesus. Mother said, "Don't you think you should have consulted me before you did it?" Dad just championed it, though. He thought it was great and said, "No, they're independent . . . they made up their own mind to do it." I said, "Chess did it, and Dan did it, and Gene did it . . . we all did it together!" Dad agreed and said, "I think they did the right thing!" Mother said, "Well, you've always talked to me before about these things, but if you really wanted to do it, I guess it's all right." We talked about it for days.

How did your mother pass away, and how did you respond to her death?

After Pappy died, Mother nursed Maa Maa for a long while. Pappy had left Maa Maa an annuity of $500 a month, which she turned over to Mother, and she lived with us for a long time. At some point, one of the relatives objected, saying that they should get the $500 a month and Maa Maa could come and live with them. After about three months of Maa Maa living with them, they couldn't stand it any longer and asked if Mother would take Maa Maa back. She did, and Mother nursed her for years and years.

After Maa Maa died, Mother lived with Sis and Brother for many years. (Dad had passed away due to a heart attack several years earlier.) Eventually, however, Mother got her own apartment in Lexington, Virginia. She had many wonderful friends who looked after her and would invite her over, and loved her so.

At the time she actually passed away, it was her heart. I was at a speaking engagement, and they told me she had passed away just before I went on. At first, I thought I couldn't do the speech, and then I thought that Mother would have wanted me to do it. I think it was a real estate group in Birmingham, Alabama, or Chicago or some big place like that. All during the speech, I could hear her voice gently encouraging me: "Cavee, Cavee . . . my little Cavee." I had a hard time getting through the speech without crying. I was very sentimental, and I had the feeling that my audience was with me and that Mother was encouraging me. I had a good reaction from the audience . . . it was very emotional.

I took a bus, then, to Lexington for the memorial service, and Mother was buried next to Dad. So many people are buried in the Lexington Cemetery because of their position — they are famous and are given all kinds of accolades. But there are a lot of other people who may not be famous but who have an incredible depth of character and a greatness within them. I don't think there is anyone I've ever known who influenced people for good any more than my mother did. So many of the students she taught just worshiped her.

Mother was a great teacher. She taught a lot more than just the nuts and bolts . . . she was really in the "people business" and influenced a lot of lives. Whenever people would have a spiritual question or would seek guidance from someone, they would come to Mother. Even her nieces worshiped her. She was really the matriarch of the whole family . . . there was no question about it.

Mother had a very loving and open-minded attitude toward spirituality. She was more of a believer in living right than in the strict Baptist religion. Dad always thought that unless you were a Baptist, you hadn't given your soul to God. But Mother didn't feel that way. She didn't argue with Dad about it, but she felt that any religion was good if you lived right. In her later years, she subscribed to *Guideposts*, published by Dr. Peale's ministry, and she attended the Unity Church when she visited us in the winters.

My mother once loaned me $5,000 when I was very sick. After I was well again, I started making a lot of money selling real estate lots. I told Mother that I'd invested some of that money and that it had just grown, grown, grown. It really hadn't, but I was making a lot of money on these real estate lots. I would tell Mother that she had so much money coming in. She got pleasure out of sending money to the grandchildren and making financial gifts to help them through school. All along, she thought she was independently wealthy. I look back and think the greatest thing I did for Mother was to give her the pleasure of feeling that she was a wealthy woman and could be generous with the kids.

17

Dad (Joseph Clark Robert)

My father was a very religious person, and he also thought you must have a pattern of life and stick to it. Grandpa, my father's father, had been married to a very charming lady, and they had two children — my dad and his brother, then she passed away. Grandpa married again and had three children by his second wife. My father's mother had left a will, and she left some money for the education of her two children: my dad and his brother. Grandpa took this money and used it for the education of the other three children. My father wanted to be a doctor very much. My grandfather said he wasn't smart enough and indicated one of the other children was the "smart" one, and he would be going to medical school. My father became a veterinarian instead.

Not only did Grandpa not give Dad the money his mother had left to him, but Dad also had to work his way through college — milking cows, making up beds — and he worked during the summer. He really had a hard life, and he always had an inferiority complex.

Back in that day and time, your parents would select who you were going to marry. My mother fell in love with her second cousin, who lived in Meridian, and they were so much in love, both of them. Back then, it was considered acceptable to marry your third or fourth cousin. My father fell in love with my mother and wanted to marry her. Maa Maa and Pappy wanted her to get married . . . back then, if you weren't married by the time you were 15 or 16, you were an "old maid." They told my mother that she should marry Dr. Robert instead of her second cousin and urged . . . practically *demanded* . . . that she do it, and so she married my father.

I admired my father very much, but I never felt very close to him. He was the kind of person who gave you certain instructions, and you were expected to live up to them. He felt that to be a good father, you should use discipline, like in the Army or Navy. He was very militaristic in his use of discipline. There were times when Dad would use a strap on me — he would punish me, saying it hurt him more than it hurt me. Of course, I didn't buy it, but I had to accept it. He did it about once a month. If I'd get home late, he would do it, or if I ate something out of the refrigerator that I shouldn't when Mother was away, he'd always say, "You come and ask me before you do it." I just couldn't adjust myself that this was justifiable punishment. When I was about 12 years old, he stopped it. It got to the point where, rather than use the strap, Dad would punish me by having me make up beds or clean the yard. He found other things that were more constructive that I had to do.

He used to always say, "This is the way my father reared me, and I think you ought to do it." When he spanked me, he would say, "You know you have done wrong . . . you violated the rules . . . and as your father, I have to punish you." Later on in his life, he developed a heart condition . . . he used to have pains. He also had rheumatism.

Dad used to tell me, "I would rather see you in a coffin than with a glass of whiskey in your hand." He never would take a drink, but finally, when he started having heart trouble when they lived in a little apartment in Lexington, Virginia, the doctor said he had to have one drink a day for his heart. Dad said, "Oh, my gosh . . . I think it's terrible that I have to drink this, but my health depends on it. I guess God wants it that way."

So, Dad would take a little drink at 4 every afternoon, just before dinner. The first few months, his conscience hurt him so much. He hated it and would drink it down and make such a big to-do of it. Finally, after a few months, he got to where he would watch the clock all day, waiting for 4 o'clock so he could have his drink! Whenever we'd see him do it, he would say, "You know, I'm only doing this because the doctor requires it, and I figure that I should do it for my health." He got so he just enjoyed it so much!

18

Dad even thought playing cards was terrible. I remember one time, Brother Ray, the Baptist minister, came to visit. Mother and all of us were playing bridge, and my Dad was so humiliated for Brother Ray to see us playing cards that he hardly knew what to do. The next day, he said, "I don't know when I have ever been so embarrassed! To think that he caught you all playing cards!" For some reason, Dad got the idea, after a while, that it was OK to play the games Yukor or Flinch, but not bridge.

Dad would always require that we be at meals on time so we could bless the food. You never ate unblessed food . . . that would be a horrible thing! Dad insisted that everybody be there at the breakfast table. As Sis and Pierre got older and stayed out late when they went on dates, it was harder for them to make it down to the breakfast table on time.

"Get up and dress . . . breakfast time," Dad would go around saying, waking us all up. Then we all had to come down for the breakfast prayer. Everything was very strict and almost military-like. Mother would go along with Dad on this because he felt so strongly about it. She would say, "It means so much to your dad . . . be sure to do it." On these things that she didn't necessarily approve of, she would say we ought to do it to help Dad.

Dad did not agree with the philosophy of certain politics at the college, so he resigned from his position. He went into insurance, Union Central Life Insurance, and he lived with that a while. He more or less sold locally, in the county and surrounding areas, to family and friends. I was just entering high school at the time, about age 13, and we would sit around the dinner table, and Dad would talk about his insurance work. He was never very successful at it.

Dad stayed with Union Central Life about a year and then decided it wasn't for him. He wanted to be very busy all the time but just didn't get along with people very well, so he wanted a profession where he wasn't so dependent on people. He was tremendously interested in bee culture and apiaries. He became one of the best in the county as far as raising bees goes.

I loved my dad in a respectful way, but not intimately. He had absorbed the philosophy from his father of the preference of age. Uncle Will was preferred over him in his family because of age — Will was the oldest. Dad had been taught that preference was always given to the oldest. I would ask why I couldn't get certain things that Pierre and Joe had, and Dad would say, "Well, they are older than you. When you get to be that age, you can have it." I always had hand-me-down clothes, because the original ones were always bought for the oldest. I could never understand why Dad felt so strongly about the sanctity of age. Being the youngest, naturally this would affect me a lot. My mother would always try to make up for it in certain ways, but Dad was very strict on this.

WHAT WAS YOUR RELATIONSHIP WITH YOUR SISTER, SADIE DUVERGNE, LIKE?

Joe was about two years older than I, Pierre was about four years older, and Sadie Duvergne was about eight years older. When I was 10, she was 18, so I revered her very much . . . because of her age and also because she was feminine. We looked up to women so much more than men.

When Mother wasn't around, I would go to Sis with my troubles. I looked upon her as kind of a mother, because she was very thoughtful to all of the siblings under her. I was much closer to her than to my brothers. She would take time to talk to me and tell me not to worry too much about Dad. "He has a lot of good qualities," she would say. I knew that she wouldn't jump to conclusions, like Dad or Mother, and I trusted her — particularly after she got married . . . being a married woman gave her additional prestige. Sis was wonderful to all of the family, and members of the family would go and live with her and Brother for a year at a time. When Brother was president of Washington and Lee University, he and Sis would entertain people like the Duponts.

19

When Sis was about 35, she started developing what the doctor called a "nervous condition," and he prescribed a drink in the afternoon to relax her. But after a while, the doctor wouldn't prescribe any more. Brother would say to me, "The doctors won't prescribe anymore, yet she requires it. Do you know how to get any alcohol?" This was, of course, during Prohibition. Down at the Sigma Chi house, people would sometimes come around and sell alcohol. I found the name of a person who sold it, and I would get it for Sis . . . it was about $5 a quart. I would go about once a week to get it, but finally, the guy selling it was picked up and put in jail. His wife, who had two little kids, stepped in and started selling it. I was told that the police knew about it, but they didn't interfere because they knew she needed the money to feed those kids.

I looked at the alcohol like medicine that Sis needed. Mother assured me at first that I was doing the right thing. But when she went to live with Brother and Sis for a while, she saw what it was doing to them and she suffered so much. Mother talked to Sis about it, but Sis would say, "Well, we do it for medicinal purposes." In that day and time, people didn't know much about alcoholism, and none of us knew how to help them.

Brother taught me freshman English at Furman University, and he gave me a definition of character that I use even unto this day. He used to call on us in alphabetical order — Raley, Riley, Robert — so we knew you only had to prepare yourself about once a month, and if you weren't going to be there, you were supposed to tell the people down the line!

I was visiting Trudy, my future wife, one night, and Raley and Riley weren't going to be in class the next day, and they didn't press the panic button. Dr. Gaines called on me. We only had about five minutes before class was to be dismissed, and I knew if I could stall that long, I'd be saved by the bell. I said, "D-D-D-Dr. Gaines, I wonder if you could give me a definition of *character* that I could write down?" He walked around the room, looked at the clock and then looked at me. He put his hand on my shoulder. He knew I didn't care what character was, but he was a kind gentleman.

Dr. Gaines responded, "Young man, I don't know . . . but I'm going to give you a definition of character that you can keep until you get one better." That was over 65 years ago, and I've never heard one half as good. Dr. Gaines said, "Character is the ability to carry out a good resolution long after the mood in which it was made has left you." He continued, "For instance, we're going to have a test tomorrow" . . . and we were . . . "so tonight when you go to bed, you will resolve to study for that test. But when 6 o'clock in the morning comes, and you put your foot on that cold, cold floor, *character* is what will make you get up anyway . . . even though the mood is gone."

WHAT WAS YOUR RELATIONSHIP LIKE WITH YOUR BROTHERS, JOE AND PIERRE?

I admired my older brother, Pierre, so much because he succeeded in the things that I was most interested in. I remember he used to let me go squirrel hunting with him. The George Rifle and the Lee Guards were the two big fraternities on the Mississippi A&M campus. They used to have rifle contests, and Pierre won a shooting contest and got a ribbon for it. I sat there watching and admired it so much. I was an ambitious young hunter, and Pierre used to let me go hunting with him. He was about four years older than I was.

I remember going squirrel hunting one time with Pierre and about six others. We all planned to meet back in about two hours. Pierre saw a squirrel, and he said, "Come here, Cavett . . . I want you to shoot him." I said, "Me?" It was such a great thrill, I didn't think he would give me preference. I shot at it once and I missed; I shot at it again and didn't get it that time, either. Pierre let me shoot a third time, and I got it. I put the squirrel on my belt, and Pierre bragged on me in front of all the other guys. He said, "I didn't get anything, but Cavett did." I think about that time and how unselfish that was of him.

I loved my brother Joe, but he was more scholarly, and I didn't have as much in common with him at that time. My dad would jokingly say that they were going to adopt another son so I would have someone to be congenial with. I used to say, "Don't get a 'readee' one," because Joe was always reading . . . very scholarly, always made straight A's. Later in life, he was president of a university.

Joe took after Uncle Will, my father's older brother, and Grandpa, their father, who were very scholarly and very brilliant. Dad and Uncle Will were children by Grandpa's first wife, who died young. Joe was about a year and 10 months older than I was.

Walter, my third brother, died when I was very young, and I don't remember him. He was about five or six years older than I was. He died of a very prominent disease at the time . . . yellow fever, I think it was. I don't have any memory at all of even seeing him.

IN YOUR YOUTH, WHO WAS YOUR BEST FRIEND?

On the Mississippi A&M campus, there were two young boys who lived next door to us, Gene and Chester Chadwick. Their father was head coach at the college. Robert Ricks and Beverly Ricks were also good friends. All of us used to play ball in the backyard on Saturday afternoons.

One of my best friends, though, was Charlie Tabb. He and his wife, Annie, our house servant, helped us with the meals. They would come every day, very early, and make breakfast for us. We all had curd, and pancakes with sorghum. Annie and Charlie stayed all day and then would go home after dark. Once a week or so, they'd also help clean the house and the yard. They lived about a mile-and-a-half away.

Charlie Tabb would take me bird hunting, and he had a wonderful bird dog. You couldn't hunt quail without a dog. A dog would trail the quail or partridges and would point . . . sometimes waiting five minutes for you to get there. Then you'd walk up, and the dog would flush the birds. Quail hunting was the fanciest of all hunting in the South, because you had to have a bird dog, and quail was a delicacy to eat.

My brother Pierre, when he was working up in Birmingham at the TCI Hospital, would come home during the Christmas holidays and bring two or three doctors down for a few days to go quail hunting. I had a bird dog called Sport, and I tried to train him all year so Pierre would be able to go quail hunting.

Now, the greatest mistake a bird dog could make was to chase rabbits. That was a shameful thing. I'll never forget one of those doctors shot at my dog. He said it was just to "sting him" and teach him a lesson for chasing rabbits. He almost killed him. Pierre never brought that doctor back again.

Charlie Tabb really knew how to train a good bird dog, though, and he always had one or two dogs. I admired Charlie Tabb and loved him like an uncle. I didn't feel anything about the fact that he was black. I realized it, but he and Annie were just part of our family as far as I was concerned. When Charlie Tabb finally died, it was just like I'd lost a member of my family.

Charlie would tell stories about hunting and so forth . . . Mother called him my "hunting father." If ever I went away during the summer, he would look after Sport while I was gone. I never observed prejudice during his lifetime. When I got a little older, while I was teaching school, I saw and read more about it.

Then there was Walter, a house servant who was very dependent on Pappy. He used to get $2 every Saturday, and that's what he was paid: $2 a week. He was very childlike . . . almost like a little kid. He and his wife, Mandy, lived about a hundred yards from Pappy's house. Pappy looked after him like a member of the family.

I remember one summer when we were visiting Pappy, he claimed that Walter had stolen a chicken. Pappy hollered and cursed at him and made such a fuss, saying, "I'm so good to you, and you stole that chicken, and now I'll never believe anything you say again. If you were hungry, you should have asked me. I would have given the chicken to you." What had really happened was that Little Auntie and Uncle Allie had come up and gotten a chicken for some company they were having. Pappy felt so bad and so horrified about it . . . he tried to find Walter that night and couldn't. When he finally found him, he gave him the day off and $5 and apologized so much to him.

There were two kinds of arrangements that Pappy had with the help he got around the farm. One arrangement was where the people were paid a certain amount for working for him, and the other was where Pappy would furnish the land to be worked, and the profits of the harvest would be split between Pappy and those farmers.

Pappy would help the people who worked for him to vote. He would sign their name, and they would mark an X beside it. Pappy had four people he helped to vote: Walter and Mandy, his house servants, and Golden and his wife, who were the sharecroppers who lived on the land. Uncle Allie and Little Auntie had 22 people working for them on their farm.

TEACHING IN 'HOG EYE'
AND OTHER CAREERS

TELL US ABOUT YOUR TEACHING POSITION IN 'HOG EYE.'

After I graduated from Ol' Miss in 1929, I went to Prairie Point . . . sometimes called "Hog Eye." I lived at Pappy's for a whole year, and I got a job teaching at Prairie Point — down where the Tom Bigby and Buddy Hatchie rivers ran together. It was known all around the area as Hog Eye, Mississippi, but was on the map as Prairie Point. It was about 20 miles from where Pappy lived, which was about five miles outside Macon.

That was the year my mother, Hal, was living in the country, looking after her mother, Maa Maa . . . my grand-mother. Mother and Dad were living on Pappy's farm. Pappy was dead by that time, and they rented out most of the land. I lived there the whole eight months I taught at the Prairie Point school. Maa Maa then passed away, of a heart attack. She was right up close to 90 years old, and living there on the farm was kind of rough. There was a lot of snow, and the only heating we had was with fireplaces.

I remember when I applied for the teaching job at Prairie Point, so many had applied for the job. That was 1929, when the big Depression was all over the United States. I heard about the job and talked to a few people about it. About 22 students had attended the school the year before, including four or so kids from the Hummer family.

I went to the county superintendent of schools . . . he was in Macon, Mississippi, and he knew my family. Of course, everybody knew everybody else in that area, and the superintendent thought a lot of my parents. It didn't hurt that my father was dean of Mississippi A&M's Agricultural Department or that my mother had been dean of a school attended by veterans who had come back from the war. The superintendent said he had to get the vote of the parents . . . that was the way they always did it . . . and that he'd let me know in about a week. I went to two or three of the families and told them I'd like to meet them and that I'd applied for the job. The superinten-dent let me know about a week later that the parents thought it was fine, and I got that job for $90 a month. It was an eight-month job.

Prairie Point was a one-room schoolhouse. It was 22 miles there and back every day, so I had to get a car. The bank loaned me $125, and I bought a second-hand car . . . a Ford. It was originally $325, but I got it for $125. Gas was about 10 or 11 cents a gallon. School was supposed to open at 8, and it took about an hour-and-a-half to get there. I'd get up about 4 in the morning. Annie, our servant, used to come and cook breakfast for me before I left.

It was dark when I'd leave, and half the time, if it rained, the lights on the car wouldn't work. I'd have to stand on the running board so I could see, then reach in to steer. For a few miles it was gravel, and the rest of the way was dirt road. I used to have more trouble getting there! A number of times, I got bogged down in the mud, but there were so many farmers along the way, and they would come and pull me out.

Almost all the kids would ride their horses to school and bring along food. One or two of the parents would drive their kids there. In the winter, we had a stove, and the parents would all send wood. The kids would fuss over who would have the honor of getting there a little early to light the stove.

I taught all the way from the first grade to the 12th grade, and I had to allocate time for each grade. It was really hard to do. But the Prairie Point students were lovely kids. I never had any trouble with discipline at all. In fact, if any of the kids got out of line, I almost had to protect them, because the others got so mad at them. They were really their own disciplinarians, and they would discipline each other for me.

I remember the kids used to bring me presents. The Hummers were the biggest beekeepers anywhere in Mississippi, and they always kept me well stocked with honey. They'd bring it sometimes in the comb and sometimes in jars. I kept all my relatives supplied with honey.

I felt like my students were my own little kids. I would let some of them come home with me on weekends or when a holiday came . . . Thanksgiving or something. My grandfather's home, where I lived, had about seven rooms and no inside plumbing . . . nobody had that on the farms. I had the car, and I'd drive the kids to spend the weekend or holiday with me.

We were like a family, and I kept in touch with those kids from the time I left at the end of the school year throughout all of their lives. I was only about 19 when I went to work there, and it was amazing that I outlived so many of them; in fact, there are only two alive today. They used to write me even after I was married. Twenty and 30 years later, I used to get letters . . . when they would have any accomplishment, they would write me. One became the attorney general of the county, and he was so proud of it and would write me about his cases. I loved that year of teaching . . . it was one of the greatest years of my life. Talk about the divinity of simplicity! Life was so simple at that time.

Then my brother-in-law, Frank P. Gaines, accepted the presidency of Washington and Lee University, and my sister, Sadie Duvergne (knowing that I hadn't saved a lot of money), asked me, "Why don't you come live up here with us, and you can go to law school at Washington and Lee?"

I remember so well Sis and Brother inviting me to come to Washington and Lee and to live with them . . . I just didn't know what I wanted to do. I thought about going back to school and maybe getting an M.A. and teaching school. I did a lot of thinking about it. I thought maybe I wanted to be a teacher.

I was offered a teaching job in Columbus, Mississippi. Of course, I had a lot of relatives there in the education world, and I wondered whether I should take that. I was offered $150 a month to teach school. I thought that seemed like a lot of money.

My cousin, Bess Swan, was going with a guy who had just finished law school, and he was in the county attorney's office in Macon, Mississippi. Bess said, "Why don't you go and talk to him about law?" I had two different interviews with him, and he told me all about the glamour of law. He was a very attractive guy, and I think he was making about $200 a month. I thought, "Oh boy, that's a lot of money!" . . . you know, I had gotten about $90 a month for teaching school at Prairie Point . . . so I decided maybe I should go into law.

TELL US ABOUT WORKING ON THE GAS LINES.

After my year of teaching at Prairie Point, I heard they were putting a gas line through Mississippi, and I got a job working on it for 40 cents an hour. I was working 10 hours a day, and I worked harder than I'd ever worked in my life. It was in Noxibee County, and I worked for three months.

The two fellows who were running the project were called superintendents. They took a fancy to me, and at the end of the summer, they offered me a job if I would move to Meridian, Mississippi. They offered me $225 a month, and this much money was unheard of at the time. I went down to Meridian, and they interviewed me and said they wanted me to work with them. They were going to make me a superintendent. I talked to Mother about it a lot, and I wrote to Brother about it . . . we all discussed it. I'd never heard of that kind of money. It was more than any of my relatives were making!

After my year of teaching at Prairie Point and working on the gas line, I'd saved about $350. Sis was going to let me live with them, but I needed another $350 to go to Washington and Lee University. I went to Mr. Yates, a relative of ours and president of the Merchant Farmers Bank in Macon, Mississippi, to see if he could help me. He was very nice and said, "I think you've made a good decision to go to law school, and I know your mother helped convince you." I said "Yes, she did," and he let me borrow, without any security at all, the $350 to go to Washington and Lee.

So you decided to go to law school at Washington and Lee University?

Yes. At the end of the Civil War, they changed the name of Washington College to Washington and Lee University. Robert E. Lee was its first president. The president's home was called the Lee Home, and each president after that lived there.

I drove all the way up to Washington and Lee University in my Ford. When I got there, I sold it for $25 because I didn't need a car on the campus, and I didn't have any place to park it. I lived with Sis and Brother (Frank P. Gaines was now president of Washington and Lee) in the president's home, and I went to law school there. I stayed in the room that Robert E. Lee died in, and the first night I was so excited, I could hardly sleep!

I took the bar exam at the end of my first year of law school. To prepare for it, I took a three-week course for about $75. A big percentage of the guys didn't pass the exam, and I remember a couple of them resented the fact that I passed it. They said the only reason I passed and they didn't was the fact that my brother-in-law was Frank Gaines, the president of W&L. Of course, that was not the reason, and I was very proud of the fact that I had passed.

During my second and third years at W&L, a fraternity brother who was a judge in Lexington, Virginia, appointed me judge in some juvenile cases. I was supposed to talk to the kids to see if they should be put on probation and then write a recommendation. I picked up a few jobs that way, but for the most part, I went to school all day and studied like the devil at night.

You tried to enlist in the Army at one point in your life, didn't you?

It was a time when it was looked upon as the patriotic thing to do . . . to sign up for the draft. Dix Price, my law partner, went in and signed up and was accepted. I went to the same office and made an application. Dix and I both applied for the legal division. The draft board wanted me to bring in a doctor's report saying I was able to serve. They asked me all these questions, and I gave them my history. Down in Mississippi, I had had all kinds of problems with my lungs. And then there were all the sinus problems I had when I lived back in New York.

Well, the board looked at the reports and turned me down. I felt very bad about it, because I wanted to be involved.

That's when I rounded up volunteers to pick cotton on weekends for the farmers . . . or sometimes we'd harvest corn or peanuts. You see, a lot of the migrant farm workers had gone into the Army, and the farmers didn't have enough people to do the work.

For about a year, I spoke to service clubs and chambers of commerce all over the state about the shortage of farm workers. We organized and had a long list of people who helped. We got the papers behind the cause, so we got good publicity. We didn't charge anything. We volunteered our time to help the farmers, and we felt this was our contribution.

NEW YORK CITY
AND 'THE RACKETS'

HOW DID YOU END UP WORKING IN NEW YORK CITY?

Milton Rogers was a great friend of my mother's. Mother had arranged for him to have a date with one of my cousins, and they fell in love. Milton always looked on Mother like his own mother and was also a close friend of Brother's. We called him "Uncle Much."

Uncle Much had gone to W&L and then moved to New York, where he became president of the American Water Works. I wrote and asked if he could get me a job, because he was well connected up there. He also knew some people at the Taft Hotel, which wasn't a very elegant hotel, but they said I could stay as their guest.

Uncle Much had given a lot of business to the Beekman, Bogue and Clarke law firm and arranged for me to have an interview with Mr. Bogue after I'd been in New York about a week. He set up an appointment for me, and I was turned over to the manager, who was a much younger fellow than Mr. Bogue. All they wanted to know was had I finished law school and did I have my diploma with me, and they started me out with $150 a month. They said I had to be there a year before I could take the bar exam. I could do research and so forth, but they wanted me to study for the bar along with it.

They were so nice . . . Mr. Bogue took me around to meet all the people. He asked where I was staying, and I told him the Taft Hotel. He said, "Don't let Mr. Beekman know you're staying there, because he'd either want you to get out of the law firm or out of the Taft" . . . Mr. Beekman owned the social register. So I moved in with Ulmer Lide, whom I had roomed with at Furman University. Ulmer — we called him "Conk" — was working at some financial institution there. He had two rooms, and I rented one from him for $75 a month.

The first thing they asked me at the law firm was, "Are you married?" I said, "No, but I'm going to get married. Trudy and her family are coming up here, and Trudy and I are going to get married at the Little Church Around the Corner. I'd love for you all to come." I had no idea so many actually would! They had seven of us in one big room at the law firm, and to my amazement, the six other "law hounds" chipped in to give Trudy and me six silver goblets for our wedding present. My mother gave us two more.

Mr. Bogue asked, "Where are you going on your honeymoon?" and I said, "Well, frankly, we're not going to be able to take a honeymoon." He called me into his office and said, "We'd like to give you a present. We'd like to give you two weeks off and a trip to Bermuda." I nearly died, I thought it was so great!

I called Trudy after I got my first paycheck and said, "I can't come down to get you, but as soon as you could come up here, I'd be grateful if we could get married." Trudy and her family arrived November 29, 1933, on the morning train after traveling all night. We got married that same day. After the wedding, the law firm handed me an envelope with a check in it. I thanked them profusely, and Trudy and I went back to the apartment. We decided the best thing to do, since we didn't have any money saved, was to use the money for groceries. We'd go down to the library and study up on Bermuda and let everyone think we went there on our honeymoon. We thought the Lord would forgive us for this . . . we needed the money!

We were very careful when we went out, because we didn't want to run into anyone from the law firm. It was a big city, but we didn't want to go down near the firm where someone might see us. So for two weeks, we lived royally on that money. You could go to double features for 10 cents and get a good meal for a dollar.

When I returned to work, everyone wanted to know all about our trip. We had taken a picture of Trudy on the train and had found out about a hotel down in Bermuda and everything. To this day, I guess nobody knows we didn't go to Bermuda!

TELL US ABOUT TOM DEWEY AND THE RACKET INVESTIGATIONS.

I'd been with Beekman, Bogue and Clarke (later, the firm became Beekman, Bogue, Leek, Stevens and Black) about six months when Mr. Bogue called me into his office. He said that Tom Dewey, the New York district attorney at the time, was doing a special investigation and was having trouble getting the finances to hire assistants. Dewey had asked five or six of the major law firms — Cadwaller; Wickisham and Taft; Curley, Keeting, Hickock and Grand; our firm and a few other big New York firms — if they would furnish a part-time assistant to work under Dewey's guidance to do a lot of investigating and research. Tom Dewey called us his young "law hounds."

It was the gangster era. The end of Prohibition had been ratified on December 5, 1933, but the mafia was still very active. These were sinister characters . . . they killed people and everything. We were permitted to carry guns, but we weren't encouraged to do it. I didn't carry a gun, but I kept one at the house. We law hounds were rather careful about our involvement, concerning ourselves with more or less the legal aspect of things: a lot of research of the law and the facts.

We were permitted to have individuals served with papers and to investigate. There were law firms down on the East Side that were involved with the gangsters and were hired to protect the people selling the dope and whiskey. So we were brought in to search out the law, the individuals and the facts.

It was a new era when Tom Dewey came into office, because he was going after so much of the law-breaking. Gangsters during Prohibition had "speakeasies," where they served alcohol and you had to have a password to get in. But even after Prohibition, Dewey needed a lot of investigating done and just didn't have enough people to do it. We law hounds would make written reports and turn the facts over to the district attorney's office.

Once a week, on Monday mornings, the law hounds would get together at Tom Dewey's office for an hour or so, about six or eight of us, with one of the officials from the D.A.'s office. He would go over things with us, ask us to check on various points of law and give us assignments. We would get direction and guidance on what they were looking for . . . and we had a lot of guidance, because there were a lot of things they wanted to know about. I did this kind of work for about a year.

Mr. Bogue always wanted me to give him a copy of the written report I turned in to the D.A.'s office. He would flatter me and tell me how wonderful it was. I don't know that the reports were that good, but Mr. Bogue wanted to encourage me. I would talk to "ol' Bogue" about things, and he even investigated one or two issues and said, "You were right about such and such." A report from one of the big New York law firms carried a lot of prestige and clout and helped the D.A.'s case.

It was more or less politics with Mr. Bogue to furnish Dewey with a young lawyer to help with the investigations.

The other lawyers in the firm used to laugh about it . . . they'd good-naturedly tease me, saying, "Well, I'm glad they didn't choose me . . . they chose you because they could spare you!" But I learned a lot about criminal law during that time.

I stayed on the payroll of Beekman, Bogue and Clarke for the first six months of the Dewey investigations. My salary had been raised to $175 a month, and when I went with Dewey, the firm raised it to $200. After six months, Dewey's whole staff seemed to like me and the two other attorneys and wanted to know if we'd be willing to stay on if they put us on their payroll. So I went on Dewey's payroll for six months to a year while working on the racket investigations.

During this time, I began having a lot of sinus congestion. The air was so damp and my sinus trouble had gotten so bad that I would come home and sit under a heat lamp to try to dry my sinuses out. Finally, Uncle Much had his very close friend, a doctor in New York, examine me. They wouldn't let me pay the fee, and they took all kinds of X rays. The doctor said, "You are not going to live much longer if you stay in this climate."

Because of my sinus problems, I had to resign. I went to Mr. Leek and told him I just didn't feel I was making a success of it. He said, "Cavett, you've been sick, and the doctors have told you that you ought to go to a drier climate." Tom Dewey's office wrote a very flattering letter that helped very much when I came out to Arizona looking for work. Those six months in New York were the best six months of my life, and the doctors who advised me to move to a warm, dry climate have been dead a long, long time!

During our time in New York, Trudy and I made great friends with several people. Percy Johnston Jr., a very dear friend, was a nephew of Uncle Much. We'd go out and spend the weekends with him in Montclair, New Jersey. We would also spend weekends with the law firm's junior partner, Jack MacNaughton, who lived out in Connecticut. We'd go out with the Feddens, and then there was Julius Forstman, a multimillionaire who had a big boat. These are just some of the friends we met through the law firm.

29

30

THE WILD, WILD WEST

How did you come to live in the wild, wild, West?

I decided that we were going to move to a warmer climate. Trudy went down to live with her family for a few months until I could get out to Arizona. I had some friends in the law firm who knew the fellow who owned the Adams Hotel in Phoenix . . . Rockwell, I think his name was. He wrote to me and invited me to stay as his guest at the Adams Hotel until I could get a job.

Everyone in the law firm couldn't have been nicer in trying to help relocate me. Someone knew Jimmy Minatto in Phoenix, and they had written him and told him that I was coming out and that they hoped he could help me get a job.

I arrived in Phoenix on a train after two nights' travel — I didn't have a sleeping berth, and I slept in my seat — on February 8, 1937, and it was snowing when I got off! The snow didn't stay on the ground very long, but it was the first snow they'd had in Phoenix in 42 years. I thought, "What in the world have I come out here for?" I took a taxi to the Adams Hotel.

Jimmy Minatto called the Ellenwood and Ross law firm in Phoenix. He had been a big client of theirs and told them I was well connected back East. He said I had been recommended highly and that he would appreciate it if they would interview me for a job. I had several letters of recommendation from the law firm in New York, so I went into Ellenwood and Ross. All the senior partners interviewed me, and I remember Mr. Ellenwood said, "I don't know how in the world anyone ever got this many recommendations . . . you must be something terrific! If you're half as good as these people say you are, we want you." They started me out at $125 a month . . . it was a lot less expensive out West than it was in New York.

Jerome, Arizona

One of the first things they told me is that they would like to send me up to Jerome, Arizona. This was my first assignment. Jerome was a little place up in the mountains. There were two big copper companies — one was United Verde, and the other was United Verde Extension. One of them was owned by Phelps Dodge, which was the biggest client Ellenwood and Ross had.

Phelps Dodge was being sued by many people who claimed that the blasting in the mines was causing all the houses and buildings to slide down the mountain. My job was to defend Phelps Dodge and say the slides had nothing to do with its company, that it was the mining of the other company, which used so much flooding and took water from under the ground, that was causing the ground to shift. I investigated the situation and would talk and meet with the different engineers involved.

After about three months, Trudy finally came out to Phoenix on a train. Ellenwood and Ross let me rent a car to pick her up. I met her in Phoenix, and we drove up to Jerome. At that time, about 15,000 people lived in Jerome because of the very active mining, and right down the hill in Clarkdale was the smelter.

I was the only lawyer representing Phelps Dodge. The opposing lawyer and the judge and engineers would sit in on all kinds of hearings. Most of us stayed at the Jerome Hotel. People would see us and say, "What is this? You people fight each other all day, and then you have dinner together and celebrate and are so friendly."

The morning after Trudy arrived, we all had breakfast together — we'd meet together every morning, the lawyers and the judge and the engineers. They had a little room there for us all in the restaurant. I was really proud of Trudy. They all asked her, "Well, what do you think of this city?" And she said, "Well, you know, the strangest thing happened last night . . . I thought it was a cyclone or something! I heard this blasting, and the hotel was shaking . . . I thought we were sliding down the hill!" Everybody started roaring with laughter. Of course, Trudy didn't know why they were laughing . . . she didn't know anything about the lawsuit.

As a result of that, I advised Ellenwood and Ross that if we could make some settlement, we should. So the president of Phelps Dodge came up. He stayed at the hotel, too, and the next day he said, "You know what you told me about what your wife said? Last night, I thought the hotel was going to slide down the hill, too. We've got to settle this lawsuit." So we settled it, as I recall, for just under a million dollars.

Soon after that, Trudy and I moved back to Phoenix for about six months. We stayed at the Westward Ho Apartments, which were owned by someone who had gone to Washington and Lee. I had to have a sinus operation, and I developed an infection and almost died. Trudy worked for the local paper, selling ad copy for the comics section to pay the bills.

There were only 42,000 people living in Phoenix at the time, and we knew so many people there. Through some connection, I got to know George Mickle, who was president of Phoenix Title and Trust Company. He was also on the board of directors of Arizona Edison Company. I had heard that Arizona Edison was looking for a lawyer, so I went to George. He said, "I'll arrange a meeting for you, but after that you're on your own." So I went to the president of the utility company and told him I'd like to apply for the job. He said he wanted to think it over. After about three days . . . I'd had some people write letters of recommendation . . . he said, "OK, but you'll have to go down to our headquarters in Douglas, Arizona." I went down to look it over, and the people were so nice down there that I came back and told them I'd like to accept the job.

Douglas, Arizona

Arizona Edison was paying about $225 a month, and they said, "The job is to be one of the attorneys, but you've also got to travel around and be public relations person for our 19 cities around the state." These included Coolidge, Casa Grande, Gila Bend, Jerome, Miami . . . little towns all over Arizona.

I was there about a month before Trudy joined me . . . she'd stayed in Phoenix at the YWCA while I set things up in Douglas. I was finally able to get a place . . . an apartment above the bank, next to the Gadson Hotel. Arizona Edison furnished me a car, and I drove to Phoenix and got Trudy. I was so afraid she wouldn't like where I was staying, because we had to walk up a flight of stairs, and it was above a branch of the Bank of Douglas.

We drove from Phoenix to Douglas, and we went through Tombstone, Arizona. At that time, it was a very tiny little place. Now it has all kinds of museums and so forth, but at that time, it was a tiny place. I drove around three or four streets, and I parked right in front of a little ol' mud hut. I said, "Now, Trudy . . . close your eyes. I hope you'll be a good sport about it. I did the best I could . . . I couldn't rent an expensive place. Here it is." Trudy opened her eyes, cleared her throat and said, "Oh, that'll be fine, sweetie . . . I know we'll get a better place some-day." I finally reached over and said, "Sweetie, I'm pullin' your leg. We're not even in Douglas . . . this is Tombstone!" She was so relieved!

When we finally got to Douglas, the little place over the bank looked like a mansion! Trudy said, "Oh, wonderful! Terrific!" I said, "But you've got to walk up steps." "Oh, I don't mind that a bit," she said. We had to take our stuff up the stairs there at night, but Trudy didn't mind a bit. That was our initial approach to Douglas.

Everyone at work was so full of curiosity about what my wife looked like. The day after Trudy arrived, Ralph Smalley, the manager of Arizona Edison, arranged to have the employees come from Bisbee and Douglas. They were all going to give a welcoming party for Trudy. We had one of the biggest parties you ever saw, and everyone thought Trudy was the greatest thing that ever happened.

We didn't stay above the bank very long. Soon, we were able to rent a furnished house. I was taking the Arizona bar exam the day our first child, JoAnn, was born. Penny Gaines, my nephew, was living with us at the time, and he took care of Trudy and took her to the hospital. Both JoAnn and Cavett Junior were born in Douglas. Our other children were born in Phoenix — Bill in 1947, and our twin daughters, Lee and Lyn, in 1950.

So my job for the next three years was visiting these cities around Arizona. I was away from home most of the time. I'd leave on Sunday night and be gone Monday, Tuesday and Wednesday, then spend Thursday, Friday, Saturday and Sunday at home. In fact, every job I've ever had, I've been away from home most of the time.

I would go into clusters of towns — Coolidge, Casa Grande and Gila Bend one week . . . Globe, Miami and Yuma another week — and I'd stay in motels, mostly. I'd hold meetings, and there were a lot of legal matters I consulted on. I'd also speak to chambers of commerce, and I spoke to the Lions clubs around the state . . . I was state head of the Lions Club. I joined the Toastmasters Club, and I would do a lot of public relations work. We wanted to keep friendly with the little-town utilities, because we didn't want them to try to take over and to have municipally owned utilities.

So, my main job was public relations, and I spoke to a lot of the churches around . . . a lot of the speeches I gave were spiritually oriented. It didn't take as much to speak back in that day and time . . . you wouldn't speak longer than 15 minutes. You take that speech I gave on character — Brother's speech. I bet I gave that speech 50 times all over the state.

The towns I spoke in weren't very big, and there wasn't very much competition in speaking. I'd go to a town, and the people would think, "Oh, he used to be with Tom Dewey!" or "Gosh, he used to teach a Sunday school class of Dr. Norman Vincent Peale's!" So, they were thrilled to have me speak . . . I was a mini-celebrity to them!

Our family stayed in Douglas about three years. Trudy didn't like it there . . . she said it smelled to high heaven of sulfur smoke. The funniest thing is that the smelter closed down while we were living there, and so many people in Douglas lost their jobs. So when they started the smelter up again, everybody would say, "What a heavenly smell!" And it smelled just terrible, but they got their jobs back, so they thought it was a good smell.

The president of the company I worked for at the time wanted me to try to sell some stock so he could get control of the shares. I got Duke Johnston and Julius Forstman, my friends back East, to buy some. They bought about 30 percent of it. The president kept bragging on me, saying, "That's fine, that's fine." He was so afraid some local people were going to buy stock and try to run the company locally. Unfortunately, the president of the company was an alcoholic, and his behavior became unpredictable. All of a sudden, he thought I was trying to take over the company, and he just got terrible. He said he was going to fire me. He was really losing control of himself and getting thrown in jail up around Globe and Miami.

Then my friends back in New York, Duke and Julius, said, "We'll buy enough stock so you can get 52 percent of it." They started buying it, and there was a big proxy fight. They bought the stock at $8 a share and turned around and were able to sell it at $18 a share. So Duke and Julius made several million on it, but I didn't let them turn the stock over to me 'cause I was so fed up with it all. We were tired of living down there in Douglas anyway, and we wanted to move back up to Phoenix.

Phoenix, Arizona

When we moved back to Phoenix, I got a job with the Industrial Commission, but soon after, I was offered a job with the law firm of Roland Hill. Eventually, we became Hill, Robert, Hill and Price.

O.C. Williams was land commissioner at that time, and he offered me a job in charge of real estate under the land department for $250 a month. There were a lot of land frauds in the real estate business all over the state at the time, and we needed to have better control. I studied the situation and told O.C. what I thought we ought to do was get a real estate act. I drafted a proposed act, and it was adopted by the state legislature. There was quite a write-up about me in *Reader's Digest* over what I had done to correct the land frauds.

I finally took over the educational division of the real estate department and was there for a good many years. I could not represent the state and practice law at the same time, so I did not practice law at this time. No real estate examinations were given until that time, so we changed the law where you had to get your license in order to practice selling real estate and pass an examination. I wrote a course and was educational director of the real estate department under the land commission.

There were very few states that had real estate acts at that time. Because I had drafted and promoted such an act through the legislature, I was invited all over the country to lecture on how we set this up so we could help other states set up something similar.

It was through real estate that I got into selling cemeteries. Before you could sell a cemetery, it had to comply with the laws of real estate. Then later, the cemetery acts would have to go through, requiring anyone who opened a cemetery to make an application, have the cemetery zoned and do a lot of other things. There were only four approved cemeteries in California. I had made the application for all four and kind of promoted the act.

There were a few other people doing this, but I was the one who started "pre-need" sales. There were all kinds of cemeteries, but there was not much promotion of them. We started this thing of selling pre-need lots. People couldn't say, "Well, I'm not going to use them." So, we developed these cemeteries and offered the sale of lots for about one-fourth the price if people bought them in advance.

In developing training for selling real estate and pre-need cemetery lots, I created courses that included records and filmstrips. Audiovisual equipment — consisting of a portable filmstrip projector that had a record player in it that played 45s — was included to assist the salespeople in their presentations. I made several courses that could be demonstrated on this equipment, and I would bring in salesmen and teach them how to use it in the selling of pre-need cemetery lots. These individuals had to get a real estate license, too.

I got four or five people involved in this plan. I'd set them up and get them approved, with the agreement that they would give me 5 percent of their gross sales. I got kind of disgusted with it, though, because they started making a lot of money and didn't want to pay me. Finally, I wrote them all and said to just give the money to charity.

ON A MORE AIRBORNE NOTE . . . TELL US ABOUT YOUR AIRPLANE.

So many people had little planes out West back then. You could land almost anywhere with those planes . . . there were a lot of little landing fields. I had a Piper Cub to begin with — just a single-prop, two-passenger model — and it would make 250 or 300 miles an hour. I never let Trudy fly with me. In fact, we would never fly together on any commercial flight while the children were young.

The fellow who sold me the plane was also a teacher, and he taught me how to fly. I got my pilot's license learning on weekends. There were certain stages of development, and I worked toward my solo flight. My instructor would show me how to do something, then he'd let me do it . . . we'd make two circles around the field.

I remember taking the plane up, and I had all the instructions. I even had instructions on how to bail out! He encouraged me and guaranteed me that he would teach me how to fly. I'll never forget how thrilled I was on my first solo flight! The first trip I ever made was down to Gila Bend. After that, I'd fly to Globe and Yuma.

We had a landing field at the bottom of Rancho Grande. I had an arrangement with a farmer that if I had to make an emergency landing, I'd call in and he would park his car, with the headlights on, right where I needed to land. One time I got into trouble, because a couple had parked there and were necking, and I thought it was the farmer with his headlights on so I could land . . . I practically crash-landed!

One time when my brother Pierre, his son Pierre Jr., Trudy and our kids came to visit Rancho Grande, they were all watching me land the plane when one of the wheels locked up. The plane spun around and around, and my young son jumped up and down, clapping his hands and saying, "Do it again, Daddy . . . do it again!"

Another close call was when Dick Harless was running for governor, and I flew him up to Globe to make a speech. When we were flying back, a terrific storm came up. I was afraid I couldn't land, so I flew around for a while. When I started running low on gas, I said, "Dick, I'm going to leave it up to you. I don't know whether I'll be able to land with the storm going on down there. I know you can jump, because you have your parachute . . . it's just a matter of whether you want to take a chance. I'm going to leave it up to you, but I believe I would advise you to jump." He said no, that he would stay in the plane with me.

We finally landed. The next day when the field pilot checked the plane, he told me I didn't even have a pint of gas left and he didn't know how I made it. I never flew the plane after that . . . I was so thankful and prayerful and lucky that nothing had happened to Dick or me. I had had several close calls by then, and when Trudy and I found out we were going to have twins, she asked me to sell the plane, and I did.

Pursuing a Speaking Career

Why did you take up speaking as a career?

Toastmasters

I'd always had a great desire to speak . . . even way back when I had that incident with the Dialect Literary Society in high school, where I was overcome with stage fright and ran from the stage. When I went to New York and practiced law, I met Ralph Smedley, who formed Toastmasters, and I was very fascinated by that organization.

I told Smedley about the incident where I ran from the stage and how I'd had such terrible stage fright as a kid. He told me nervousness was an asset rather than a liability and said you could never be a good speaker if you looked at it as just sort of a routine thing, with a "six-of-one/half-dozen-of-the-other" kind of attitude. He said that if you were so excited about making a speech and considered it so important that you were nervous about it, then you had that great desire to be excellent.

I was a member of the Young Lawyers Association, and I brought several of the young lawyers into Toastmasters International. The course influenced me so much that I entered the International contest in 1941. I won the local contest, then the district, and I came in second in the International contest that year.

I asked Ralph Smedley why it was that I came in second . . . what my shortcomings were. He said, "Cavett, if you had given a story, a signature story, I believe you would have won. There is nothing more powerful or more persuasive than giving a story to illustrate your point." Smedley's whole philosophy was that you had to "have a message crying for expression, riding on the wings of humor to make it digestible, with stories to remember it by." So, I entered the contest again the next year, having spent the whole year in between working on a story and getting ready for my talk. The story I finally developed was The Whiskey Story. I worked so hard on it.

The competitions took place right after the war, in 1942, and I won the local, the division and so forth. When I got down to the finals, they called them off because of the war. Instead, they wanted to have all participants go into a recording studio and record their speech on a record and send it in, then deliver it in person later. Recording a speech was something new back then. For the contest, you could give it only once, and I brought a bunch of people into the studio to be my audience. It was then, in August of 1942, that I won the Toastmasters International contest with The Whiskey Story. Smedley told me that if I hadn't given that story so beautifully, I wouldn't have won it. He said, "We went over and over and over the speeches, and we all agreed that The Whiskey Story was why you won it." Here's the script to that speech.

THE WHISKEY STORY

Down in my native state of Mississippi — down in the old Bible Belt, down where Prohibition still has its strongest citadel — I read not too long ago of an incident that illustrates a point I want to make here tonight. The local editor of the *Macon Beacon*, a little country paper in Noxibee County, had the unadulterated gall to ask a local politician — during a campaign, mind you — how he stood on the "whiskey question."

What a horrible thing to do to anyone in the state of Mississippi who's running for office! You see, you'll be damned if you do and be damned if you don't. If you say, "I am *for* whiskey," you will get half of the votes and you will lose half. If you say, "I'm *against* whiskey, you will lose half and get half. And if there are over two candidates in the race . . . my friends, you're in a bad, bad way.

But I thought this local politician acquitted himself in a most admirable fashion, because this is what he wrote back to the paper. He wrote back, and he said, "Sir, I had not planned to discuss this controversial question at this time, but far be it from me to sidestep any issue, regardless of the nature and regardless of the results. But I want to be sure I understand you now, sir.

38

"If, sir, when you say 'whiskey,' if you mean that devil's brew, that poison scourge, that bloody monster that defiles innocence, dethrones reason, creates misery and poverty — yea, takes the very bread out of the mouths of babes . . . if, sir, when you say 'whiskey,' if you mean that vile drink that topples the Christian man and woman from the pinnacle of righteous and gracious living into the bottomless pit of despair, depravation, shame, hope-lessness and helplessness, destroys homes, creates orphans and depraves the community in general . . . sir, if that's what you mean by 'whiskey,' I want you to put in your paper that I promise my constituents, if I am elected, I'll fight to destroy this demon with all the strength I possess."

"BUT IF, on the other hand, when you say 'whiskey,' if you mean that oil of conversation, if you mean that philosophic wine and ale that's consumed when good fellows get together, puts a song in their hearts, laughter on their lips, warm contentment in their eyes . . . sir, if you mean that medicinal spirit that puts a spring in the ol' man's step on a frosty morn, if you mean that nectar of the gods the sale of which puts untold millions in our treasury, tenderly cares for our little orphan children, the blind and the deaf, the halt and the maimed, the aged and infirm . . . yea, verily builds great highways, schools, hospitals and makes this world a better place in which to live . . . now, sir, if that's what you mean by 'whiskey,' I want you to put in your paper that I promise my constituents, if I'm elected, I'll fight to protect this essence of divinity with all the strength I possess."

■   ■   ■

Then I thought he added the crowning climax, the capstone of it all. He said, "Sir, now that I've answered your query without equivocation, I hope you will, in good conscience, put in your paper that I am a man with the courage of my convictions. This is my stand. I will not compromise . . . this is my stand."

The reason I like that story is this: You and I differ on a lot of things, and that's just the way it should be. You see, if you and I agreed on everything, one of us would be unnecessary . . . I don't know which. But there's one thing that everyone here agrees upon, or you wouldn't be here tonight. And that is, whether a person is an introvert, extrovert, megalomaniac, Caspar Milquetoast, octogenarian, child prodigy, doctor, lawyer, merchant, chief, priest, prophet, pawnbroker or peanut vendor . . . my friends, we're in the PEOPLE BUSINESS. Every one of us is seeking to cause the other person to think and then feel and then act as we desire.

You see, the doctors are trying to persuade their patients, the lawyers are trying to persuade the juries, the pastors try to persuade their congregations, lovers try to persuade their sweethearts. We don't have the same approach, our end results are not the same. But everybody asks, "Who will be influenced by me?" Yes, this is the day of professionalization.

When we talk about professionalization today, we mean not only the category of performance but also the quality of performance. Any society today that would ignore quality in plumbing because plumbing might be considered a humble activity or that would tolerate shoddiness in philosophy because philosophy might be considered an exalted activity will not have either good philosophy or good plumbing . . . neither its pipes nor its theories will ever hold water. Yes, today is truly the day of professionalization, and the professional has to not only *tell* his ideas but also *sell* his ideas.

Through this victory in the Toastmasters International contest, I got many invitations to speak. They were more or less freebies, but I got good exposure.

I've been privileged to be a member of Toastmasters for over 60 years, and it's just amazing to me how all the different clubs seem to have personalities of their own. The Park Central Group that I'm currently involved with has a different personality because its membership consists of people who are professional speakers and who have been in business for a long time. Some groups have members who have just gotten out of school and are starting out. But my group has had a lot of experience, and the members stimulate each other . . . they give such good suggestions on how to improve.

WHEN DID THE VISION TO BECOME A SPEAKER GRAB YOU?

It didn't happen all at once. It gradually was born, then started growing up and finally, it reached maturity and became a vision . . . and then I never got rid of it! I once heard that there is a law of life as strong as the law of gravity and as old as time itself. It was old when they floated the stones down the Nile . . . it was old when this country was born. It's the law of displacement. When you get anything of value in life today, you later will look back and realize you had to give up something in order to get it.

When I finally had a vision to become a great speaker, it replaced all the dried pablum of academic theory and little principles that I tried to learn about public speaking: always have a good opening, get the audience's attention, tell a good story. I didn't have to think so much about the structure of a speech — it was your message and your audience that mattered. It's like painting a beautiful painting, or sculpting clay and molding it. Whenever you get to the point where you fall in love with your audience and feel your message strongly . . . those two things . . . that's when you know you've arrived.

HOW DID YOU GET STARTED IN PROFESSIONAL SPEAKING?

I had been speaking to service clubs and Toastmasters groups and chambers of commerce all along . . . during the time I worked with Arizona Edison, when I was with the Arizona real estate department and when I practiced law. In 1941, I entered the Toastmasters International contest and came in second. The next year, I won the contest. It takes more to win a state contest now than it did to win the national back then.

Although I had spoken to civic groups, service clubs and churches for many years after joining Toastmasters International in New York City, it was quite a while before I made any money speaking. John Hammond invited me to speak to the group called International Sales Marketing Executives in Boston, Massachusetts. He announced at that meeting that I was available to speak to groups for $150, and afterwards, I was invited to 18 future speaking engagements. Every time I spoke after that, I was invited to speak to two or three other groups.

At speaking engagements, I'd sell my record albums on the subject of sales, and I'd make $10 in album sales for every dollar I made speaking. People used to ask me if I really made that much money on my albums. Let me put it this way: I would agree to speak for free if attendance was estimated at 100 or more people . . . just so I could offer my educational materials!

Back when I was 61 and went into it, speaking was a very personal thing. Except for a few pastors and retired politicians, speakers weren't routinely invited to speak to a group every month or every six months . . . usually, someone would know you, or you had a friend in the organization. So it was more of a personal thing. Now, of course, a new profession has been born with the speakers bureaus, and there's an increased demand for speakers.

Over half the speaking engagements I got in the beginning were from the real estate industry, and this was because I had worked in real estate. The same was true for insurance, because I had been in the insurance field. One of the very first speeches I made was for the California Real Estate Association, and I got many invitations as a result of that speech. I came home and asked Trudy, "You mean people will pay for this?" and Trudy said, "Apparently, they will." Then I asked her, "Would you mind if I went into this to see if I could make a living at it?" And she said, "I think you'd be very good at it."

There was no way for things to get routine with speaking, because every audience was different and no course had been set. When I first attempted to enter the field, I made every mistake that had ever been made . . . in fact, I believe I invented a few new ones! These were totally uncharted waters . . . it was a profession being formed, and I learned by doing. I started running large ads, sending out hundreds of free cassettes, going around the country calling on program chairs . . . experimenting in every respect. Would you believe that my first year, I spent $23,000 more than I took in? The second year, I spent $18,000 more than I took in.

Because I had taken the Dale Carnegie course and had studied Toastmasters with Ralph Smedley, when I first went into this thing, I was more or less thinking to myself, "How could I imitate those people?" Finally, somewhere down the line, the opportunity in front of me got an emotional grasp on me, where I felt this was a chance to do more than just teach principles . . . I started figuring I wanted to make a difference in people's lives. It wasn't just a matter of teaching them the ABC's and so forth. *You've got to get their attention, you've got to get their interest, and you've got to get their action.* I was glad to see audiences embrace the principles, but when I really got a kick out of this thing . . . when it really wrote itself indelibly in my heart . . . was when I saw the difference it made in their lives. Those are two different things: teaching people things and seeing those things affect their lives.

WHAT WAS ON YOUR MIND WHEN YOU WERE TRAVELING *250* DAYS A YEAR? IN RETROSPECT, WAS IT FOOLISH OR WAS IT GREAT?

Well, to begin with, I think I appreciated and enjoyed the recognition that I was a successful speaker. I would get up and watch people react to the ideas that I would have and become excited by their reaction. But the longer I spoke over the years, I wasn't as concerned about the money I was being paid or the recognition I was being given. I started getting to the point where I got a great sense of satisfaction from the feeling that I made other people's lives easier and sold people on certain principles that they were adopting.

So, it was kind of a transition, and I think that's the way it is with so many speakers today. They start out all excited . . . glad they are making money, getting recognition and getting the greatest pleasure out of seeing people give them a standing ovation. But the longer you stay in the field of speaking, the more you get satisfaction from the feeling that you're making a difference in the lives of other people. You're teaching them to be happier, to be more successful and to carry on the thing that you are carrying on — that is, to help other people in life. In other words, you get to the point where you have earned the right to be accepted because of what you've done for other people rather than for yourself.

It was only a few years ago that I realized the greatest force you can help people develop is the power to work for their success. Previously, I bought the idea that it was self-fulfilling prophecy — that you'd put a photograph of a Cadillac on your wall and say, "I want to earn that, to be worthy of that, to feel like I have a right to have that." And that's all right, that's fine. But that is really just an elementary thing. When you mature enough and have had enough experience, you know that the greatest force you can ever give people to help them work harder and be more successful is to help them know you believe in them — that's *creative expectancy* . . . you believe in them.

WAS THERE ANY POINT DURING YOUR SPEAKING CAREER WHERE YOU FELT YOU WERE OVERDOING IT BY SPEAKING *200* DAYS A YEAR?

That's a very easy question to answer. At the height of my acceptance by audiences, when I was about 75 years old, I got to the point where I was accepted so beautifully at times that I just took it for granted. That's the time I had my first heart attack. I was speaking before a group when my message became all clouded. I couldn't understand it, and I had to stop and say, "Folks, I have a problem . . . I'm sick. But," I continued, "there's a brilliant person in this audience . . . Joe Klock has some ideas that you need right now, and I know he'll rise to the occasion and help you." I bragged on him, and Joe later said he would've died before letting me down. He told me that so many people called him and said, "That was really great how you took over." He said he could trace several later speeches back to that incident and told me how impressed people were that he could just take over like that. He did, and he did a beautiful job. I will always be grateful to him.

I realized then that I had to quit speaking 200 times a year, but I put more stress on the times I did speak. I prepared more and came to realize that I didn't have to climb the rhetorical heights of ecstasy with each speech. I got out and was really interested in trying to help people live better lives, and I gave a message teaching them to get away from the dried pablum of academic theory. I came to figure that one of my greatest blessings ever was when

41

I had that heart attack. I had to change my whole attitude. I came to realize that delivering speeches wasn't so much about giving brilliant ideas that I got from books and all . . . it was about the heart-to-heart feeling that let people realize how important it was that they live a better life.

Since then, I've found out that even though I don't feel as brilliant, I feel that I can give "heart appeal" — I can be the message a little more *myself* rather than try to give *ideas* that are the message. You go through a period in life when you figure YOU are the message, and you ask yourself, "What are the important things in getting people to live better and in helping people, and how do I let people know that I know they can do it?"

Dr. Peale was a master at this. I was traveling in the Far East with him on a speaking tour, and Ruth, his wife, had set up prayer breakfasts in different areas. I'll never forget an incident at one of the prayer breakfasts, where a 14-year-old girl made my whole trip over there worthwhile when she got up, put her hands together, looked up and said, "Dear God, help me to be the kind of person my dog thinks I am."

Believing in people is the most powerful motivating force there is. Concentrating more on each speech helped me connect more with the people and let them know I believed in them.

SO, IT TOOK YOUR BODY'S SHUTTING DOWN TO GET YOUR ATTENTION AND TO MAKE YOU REALIZE, "I GUESS I'M OVERDOING IT"?

A great part of my life, I guess I have to admit, I was kind of jealous of my brother-in-law and my brothers and so forth. They were great speakers. They'd get out and get all kinds of standing ovations, and I always wanted to be as great as they were. The time in high school when I ran from the stage when I couldn't remember my speech . . . that scenario made me feel so insecure. I wanted so much to be a brilliant speaker.

Many years later, I got to a point in my speaking career where I was getting all kinds of recognition and standing ovations and more invitations than I could fill. But I wasn't as ambitious from my heart, as I became later . . . not as concerned about getting the right message over. I wanted to say the things that would get me acclaim and so forth. After I had the heart attack and couldn't speak at all for a while, I kept wanting to get back. As I studied and tried and prayed that I could, it was just the important things that would come back to me.

Now, I'm not criticizing other people, but I see so many speakers coming along with a whole volume of ideas, and it seems like the ol' idea of "burning down a house to roast a pig." Later in their lives, many speakers get to the point with their messages where it's kind of like the cream rising from the milk. They may give fewer ideas, but the ideas are a lot more important. As I went along, I got to the point where I wanted to give my audiences just the cream, not skim milk.

Now, I think you have to have that volume of ideas in the beginning . . . just as you've got to have all of the milk in order to get the cream. But the longer you stay in speaking, the more clearly you see the ideas that people react to, and you have better judgment. I think one of the greatest things that can ever happen is when you realize you have ideas, and they go into judgment, and finally, a few things go into wisdom. As you go through that process, you have fewer ideas, but they are much more important.

So, when I went back into speaking after my heart attack, I think I really had better material. I was only using the things I felt were important for people to help them live a better life — I got away from the "know-how" and concentrated on the "do-how." I realized the importance of becoming the message yourself. If you've been in the business 20 years, you find out that you use a much smaller number of ideas than you did in the beginning, but they are better, heavier and more helpful to other people.

WHEN YOU FIRST LOOK OUT ON THE SEA OF FACES IN AN AUDIENCE, HOW DO YOU GET CONTROL OF YOUR FEAR?

One of the ideas I finally bought is that if you do not get excited over your audience, you are not going to do a good job. As Ruth Peale said about her husband, "The only time I'm frightened that my husband isn't going to do well is when he doesn't get all excited. When he's excited and a little nervous, he puts forth his best effort."

For a long time, I was afraid when I would get nervous. But then, there are a lot of ways you can overcome that. One thing I do is know my speech so well that I can get through the first few paragraphs without making a mistake. I rehearse the first part of my speech more than any other part. Some people have other ways — for instance, I heard someone say that they imagine the audience in their underwear. Maybe that helps some speakers get beyond feeling intimidated by their audience.

I've tried to adopt the philosophy that I learned from Ralph Smedley, the founder of Toastmasters International. When I get up before an audience, the first thing I think is, "Is this 'Here I am' or 'There they are'? Am I going to try to show off, or am I going to really try to get through to them?" Whenever I get up there and get myself in a mood of giving ideas to help people and thinking of their problems . . . and divorce myself from my own feelings . . . I find that I get through to my audience better and speak with more authority, and I really enjoy it.

I once asked a speaker, "When does a speaker become a professional?" And his answer was, "When he or she gets to the point of enjoying the speech even more than the audience does!" In other words, if I'm enjoying it, the audience is going to enjoy it. So, I want to be sure I believe in my speech enough that I'm enjoying getting the message through. Then I know the audience will grab it.

I like to have a speech so firmly in my mind that I can hardly wait to get to every little point of it . . . I am *attracted* by it. If I had to stop and think, "Now, let me see . . . what do I say next?" it would create a vacuum where fear could come in. I see my outline and the four or five points way ahead, because they are so fixed in my mind. If I don't have enough time, I can skip a point or two. If I have my mind fixed on something and I know it's good, I can hardly wait to get there . . . it crowds out any fear. The only time you have fear is when you have a vacancy and don't have a powerful message you want to give.

When I speak, I actually see words and a "picture map" in front of my eyes . . . I know my speech that well. I usually start out with the Dizzy Dean story or my story about the Yanks, so I see a little baseball bat at the top. Then I go into my old Irish legend with four people: I see a little square under the baseball bat, with the corners named Everybody, Somebody, Anybody and Nobody. Then I talk about the paycheck, and I see a paycheck. When I talk about addressing a group in Hawaii, where they gave me a luau, I see a hula dancer . . . and on and on. I visualize these parts of my speech in pictures and words so I can actually see a map in front of my eyes or on the wall behind my audience. In this way, I don't have to put energy into remembering the words; I can see the speech and concentrate on connecting emotionally and mentally with my audience.

There is a difference between fear and anxiety or excitement. If you don't consider your audience or the situation important enough to make you a bit anxious, then it's too bad — it's a blessing to have it. You'll never be a great speaker unless you have the excitement that comes from the ambition to do a good job. When the adrenaline flows, it helps give you an energy and a peak performance that you could never even rehearse for.

The issue, then, is how to *deal with* the fear, anxiety, excitement . . . *not* how to get rid of it. That is a very important idea. You don't want to get rid of the butterflies in your stomach . . . you just want to teach them to "fly in formation"!

43

Another way I control fear is to always have one or two ideas in my hip pocket that can be applied to almost any situation. One of the things I say these days is, "My feelings are so much stronger than anything I have to say that I want to give the brilliance of silence!" Having one or two ideas that are versatile enough to apply to almost anything . . . in case you're called on to say a few remarks extemporaneously . . . is like having a little insurance policy. Even if it's a simple idea, state it with authority, as though it's important.

HOW DID YOU MEMORIZE ALL THOSE QUIPS?

Well, I'll tell you . . . repetition is the greatest thing in the world for writing something indelibly, engraving something deeply and etching something into every fiber of your being. I found out that repetition was the best way in the world to give a speech from my heart.

When I would go to bed at night and before I went to sleep, I would run through my talk in my mind, trying to give the wording of things, in particular, my attention. I would do the same thing when I woke up in the morning — while my mind was fresh, before I got out of bed. It's amazing . . . those times when your mind is alert, it takes less practice to write things indelibly into your mind than if you sit down and try to practice it when your energy is low.

Often, to make speeches part of me . . . so I could give the words from my heart and not just my mind . . . I would record them on a little portable tape recorder, then listen to them while driving or relaxing at home. I would review them when I was taking a bath or getting dressed, before I went to sleep or when waking up in the morning.

I used to sit out in the sun in Arizona to dry up my sinuses, and I would listen to my taped speeches, going over and over and over them to get them into my subconscious. I could turn the recorder on and be thinking of something else or just be lying or sitting there, and the words made an imprint on my memory even if I wasn't actively listening to them, because subconsciously, they were becoming part of me.

Then, when I actually sat down to try to memorize the speech, the effect seemed so much greater because it was kind of a dual situation . . . I'd imprinted my mind both consciously *and* subconsciously. I got the ideas vocally, mentally and through the ear. Your mind doesn't know whether you are actually delivering a speech or just listening to it on a tape recorder, so I could turn my relaxation time into learning time by using "spaced repetition" until the speech was burned into my backbone and I could give the ideas from my heart. You get to the point where you kind of live with a speech — it really becomes a part of you.

When someone tells a signature story, which I think is the most impressive thing about any speech, you can pretty much tell whether the person has lived with that story. You never get to where you tell such a story in a "canned" way . . . you tell it a different way every time because you've *lived* it, you've *experienced* it yourself. I think if you just try to memorize the words and not harmonize with it, it's never as good.

If you've been in the business as long as I have, you have one-liners that apply to every facet of your speech. Take my speech You Can't Heat an Oven With Snowballs . . . there are three points in there. I have one-liners and stories that apply to each point. They're not hard to remember, because each applies to the point I'm trying to make. Take the part of my speech that says, "You've got to know what you're doing" . . . I think of two or three little one-liners I want to give there. You've got to have knowledge — knowledge of people.

I say you can have all the dried pablum of academic theory — you can have synergism, cognitive dissonance, Maslow's theory, cybernetics, transactional analysis — but it doesn't mean a thing unless you can apply those principles to people. I don't care how smart you are, the only way in the world you are going to get through to people is by letting them know you are interested in their problems . . . by becoming a problem solver. And the only way to find out their problems is to ask questions; *whoever asks questions controls the situation.*

For instance, my wife, Trudy, bless her heart . . . I've never won an argument in my life from my wife, because she never argues — she just asks questions, asks questions, asks questions. I came home the other night, and here was a bill for a new dress. I hit the ceiling. I said, "Sweetie, you know I'm not chintzy, but not another dress this month?" Did she argue? No, she's a pro. She said, "Honey, you know when we were out the other night and you said how beautiful Ann looked? Now, you want me to look as nice as Ann, don't you?" Now, if I say "no," I've bought a whole new set of problems. But if I say "yes," I've bought shoes, bag and hat to match.

Even my little granddaughters have learned from their grandmother . . . they never argue, they just ask questions. Once when they were visiting me, one of them asked, "Granddaddy, can I have a Coca-Cola?" I said, "No, Sweetheart . . . it'll take your appetite." Did she argue? No, she's a pro. Very sweetly, she said, "Granddaddy, may I ask you a question?" "Sure, Sweetheart," I replied. "Why does a martini *increase* your appetite and a Coke *takes* mine?" she asked. All I could say was, "Shut up and drink your Coke!" Whoever asks questions controls the situation.

As for becoming a problem solver, you've first got to know what the problem is. For many years, I didn't know what a "problem" was — it's the difference between what someone's got and what he or she wants. Solving problems is just this simple: Find out what people have and what they want, and bring the two together.

I once heard someone say that you can be a walking encyclopedia of technical knowledge, but it means nothing if you don't know how to get your message through. And there's only one way to do it: You've got to let people know you're interested in their problems.

45

WHERE DID YOU GET YOUR QUIPS AND ONE-LINERS, AND HOW DID YOU INCORPORATE THEM INTO YOUR SPEECH?

I used to collect one-liners and ideas from people I would hear and admire. Trudy would give me a lot of stories, one-liners and ideas from reading that she's done. If I liked an idea, I would write it down in a little notebook I'd carry around with me in my coat pocket. If the idea applied to one of the principles I spoke about, I might try out a one-liner or story in a low-risk situation . . . maybe with family or friends. Then I would try it out in a low-risk speaking situation, and if it got a good response, it might become part of my regular speech.

When I had my first heart attack and went into the hospital, I got quite a lot of good material from that experience. At the hospital, they gave me a private room with a public nightgown and a choice of three sizes for the nightgown: long, medium and don't-reach-for-the-cookies! One of my friends sent me a nice get-well card that said he had good news and bad news for me. The good news was that when I got out, he had 12 dancing girls to entertain me; the bad news was that they were all my age!

I would write these one-liners in my little pocket notebook, and after I filled it up, I'd throw it into a box. My first book was written entirely from little pocket notebooks filled up with ideas, stories and one-liners that I threw into a box and saved.

Anytime I'd get a real gem, I'd write it down in my pocket notebook *and* in a bigger notebook. Then I would think, "How am I going to use this?" I would have certain categories, and I knew it would fit into one of those. Usually, the thing that would attract me to an idea or phrase was its beautiful language . . . I was impressed as much by the language as by the thought or principle.

■   ■   ■

I used to get hundreds of these quips and one-liners. Even now, I can look back and associate so many of them with the people I got them from. For instance, one of the last new quips I introduced into my speech was incorporated into my ending toast. Dr. Peale said, "Things people do for us die with us, but things we do for others live through all eternity." I can never say that without thinking of Dr. Peale.

When I was writing my speech called Let George Do It, I read so many little gems, I decided to put them all together. I'd use that speech when I talked to chambers of commerce to try to persuade them to become more involved. The thing I would have to fight against more than anything is using all of my favorites at once — four or five instead of just one! The favorites are like gems in a treasure chest . . . so beautiful, you want to give all of them!

HOW CAN I BECOME A PROFESSIONAL SPEAKER?

A lady called me once and said, "Look, I've been successful in the sales business, and everybody tells me I should become a speaker . . . and told me I should come to you." I gave her a copy of *Toastmasters* magazine and told her I thought she ought to join Toastmasters. I added that if she feels she's already an accomplished speaker, then she should join the National Speakers Association and become an active member of her local chapter by volunteering to be on committees. I told her she could learn more from seeing other people speak than from reading a book or getting ideas from any one person. It's a *process*.

A lot depends on getting into the right field and preparing yourself. The first thing is to research carefully and find a field that isn't overcrowded — one that needs a new speaker. Ask yourself: Am I qualified to do it? If not, how can I get myself qualified? Do I believe in it? Am I dedicated enough to stick with it? You've got to learn to have your message riding on the wings of humor to make it digestible, with stories to remember it by.

Even if you are gifted, you must always be improving yourself. You must create a speech that you work on and enjoy to the point where, as Dr. Norman Vincent Peale says, you enjoy it as much as your audience does. You must know you are a pro and be as enthusiastic as your audience is to hear your speech. You are the message, and you must develop a signature story or two that convey this.

WHAT MAKES YOU SO SURE THAT HUMOR IS IMPORTANT IN A SPEECH?

I was so impressed when I heard Will Rogers talk. He had a powerful message but clothed it in humor to make it digestible. I don't care how brilliant an individual is, if that person doesn't give his or her ideas to you in an entertaining way, those ideas are not going to be accepted. I was so impressed with Will's speech that I really tried to pick up that philosophy of speaking, and I've followed it all my life.

ASIDE FROM PERSONAL REFERRALS, WHAT DO YOU BELIEVE IS THE BEST MARKETING TOOL FOR BUILDING A SPEAKING CAREER?

As a major premise, develop the idea that, "You've got to circulate to percolate . . . you've got to make contacts to make contracts." Also, brainstorm this question: How can I reach the *most* people for the *least* cost? You don't have to do it all yourself. If you write an article and can get it printed in a publication that has a large circulation, you might reach 10,000 people. That's more efficient exposure than if you had tried to contact that many people individually.

TELL US ABOUT THE SUITCASE FULL OF MONEY IN ALASKA.

In the early 1970s, I went to Alaska and made quite a bit of money selling my books and cassettes. I was speaking to chambers of commerce and insurance companies, primarily, and you wouldn't believe how many people bought cassettes! I found out the reason the tapes were so successful up there was that I had no competition. I'd have an audience of 200 or 300 people and would sell cassettes to three-fourths of them!

People weren't using bank cards much up there at the time. They would pay for everything in cash . . . they even preferred paying in cash to paying by check. I don't think I ever experienced another place or time where people preferred to deal with cash as much as up in Alaska. I had a little suitcase in which I brought a few books with me. After I sold the books out of there, I would use the suitcase to hold the money from my book and cassette sales. I always carried the suitcase with me, and at one point, I had over $1,000 in there in $5s, $10s and $1s . . . the bills were just packed in there.

Of course, the airline people wanted to look in the suitcase, and when they saw its contents, they didn't know whether to let me through or not! So they sent for the fellow in charge to come over and decide whether to search me. I showed them my identification and told them I was a speaker. Finally, the thing that made them let me through was a brochure with a big picture on it of me speaking. When they saw this picture, they almost bowed, and they let me through! That's the story of the suitcase full of money in Alaska.

IF YOU HAD TO LIVE YOUR PROFESSIONAL LIFE OVER, WHAT WOULD YOU DO DIFFERENTLY, AND WHY?

To start with, I would try to simplify . . . I would try to live by the divinity of simplicity. After I had taken Dale Carnegie's course and joined Toastmasters, I decided that speaking and training were so challenging that I wanted to get into that type of business myself. Merlyn Cundiff and I formed the Phoenix Summer Sales Seminar, which was very successful in a small way. If I had to do it over again, I would realize that the organization would grow and grow, and that we had planted the seeds for growing the National Speakers Association. But I didn't realize how important it was at the time. Had I known, I would have spent more time in it, stayed longer and devoted 95 percent of my time to it rather than maybe a third of my time, which is what I did. Now I see how important it was and what an opportunity it was. It was important not only for me, but for the public.

In the beginning of my speaking career, I was almost apologetic when people would ask me what I did for a living. I would say, "Oh, well . . . I, uh, hold meetings." They would say, "Yeah, but what do you *do* for a living?" I would say, "Oh . . . I, uh, try to teach people how to get along in their business." "Well," they would say, "do you know the business you are trying to help them with?" "Well," I would respond, "I'm trying to help them get along with people." People didn't buy that back then, and I almost had to defend myself.

After years of success and failure, trial and error, I realized that first and foremost, speakers are in the "people business." People don't care how much you know until they know how much you care — that is the essence of the people business. I still think the greatest thing I ever heard was from this fellow who was head of the American steel industry . . . he said that only 15 percent of our success was due to our technical knowledge and 85 percent was based on our ability to deal with people. To respond to your question, what I would want to do differently would be to learn more about how to deal with people.

HOW IS PROFESSIONAL SPEAKING TODAY DIFFERENT FROM WHAT YOU ONCE IMAGINED IT WOULD BE?

Competition is a great factor in speaking today. In fact, it's hard to get speeches yourself . . . bureaus and agents have become a big part of our business. At one time, 50 or 60 years ago, the only people who spoke around were retired politicians and pastors, some lawyers and people who had made a name for themselves in fields other than

47

speaking, and audiences would turn out to see if they were stunning people. Now, the competition is much greater, and conditions have changed so much.

Take my own life, for example. I was a million-dollar producer with Union Central Life Insurance Company over half a century ago. People today are not interested in a person who can tell them how to solve problems that existed back in that day and time. They want someone who knows the problems of today and how to solve them with the facts that exist now. That's one of the greatest changes that has occurred. You can't get up and boast about what you did half a century ago and how you overcame obstacles back then. Problems have changed — that's history! Now, people want someone who the kids can relate to because of what the problems are now. In other words, there have been changes in both conditions — competition and new problems — as well as changes in ourselves as our life conditions evolve.

In addition, I could never have imagined that speaking would become the profession it has become today. I knew they had an American Bar Association and an American Medical Association, but I never thought speaking was big enough and glamorous enough to be considered a profession in and of itself.

That's why I was amazed when we finally realized it was growing, growing, growing. Dr. Peale was the one who said, "Cavett, the time has come, I think, when we [the National Speakers Association] ought to incorporate." (It had been tried twice and failed.) He told me, "There isn't anything that can't be accomplished when the right people are swept up in a worthy cause, divorced from who gets credit for what." He said, "If you get in this thing and stay with it, I'd admire you for staying with it, because it's been tried before. One time, I think they got 18 people; another time, I think they got 30. But the whole thing was organized so that those individuals who formed it could get personal benefit from it. If you do it and stay with it, I promise I will help you if you ever call on me." That was why I called on him to come speak at the NSA convention in New Orleans, and his wife Ruth made sure he did do it.

WHAT DO YOU FEEL ARE THE CURRENT TRENDS IN THE SPEAKING INDUSTRY? THE FORECAST FOR THE COMING DECADE?

I think that large corporations, rather than sending their people to big conventions, now feel training is so important, they will bring people in to train staff in-house. So, speakers must be prepared to really *train* people, not just come in with a bunch of academic ideas . . . the kind of things you'd read in a book or an article. Employers want real-life principles that employees will be able to apply.

As speakers and trainers, we're in the "people business," and there is nothing more valuable to a company than someone who can come in and train their people. We need to find out what their problems are and qualify ourselves to solve them. Today's companies demand trainers who understand what their problems are, who specialize in that field and even know their people fairly well. If you look around at the trainers who are really successful now, you'll find that most of their jobs involve going back to the same companies — in kind of a consulting role.

The training need is so big now that when you go in and give generalized training, it's just not enough. Companies want to bring in someone who is more or less in harmony with them — preferably, someone who's been in that kind of business before and has been successful at it . . . it's a more personal approach. You find out what the problems are first, the way a doctor asks a patient, before making a diagnosis, "What are your symptoms?"

WHY ARE THE GREAT SPEAKERS GREAT?

I admire some speakers so much if I know they started from scratch and overcame obstacles they had. You see, if an individual like [NSA past president and Cavett Award recipient] Nido Qubein — who didn't have a lot of money to start with and had to learn certain principles — proves that he or she can accomplish something, that is really great. I don't believe I would ever admire or want to learn from someone who didn't go that route.

What makes a great track coach? He was once accomplished at the sport himself. A great baseball coach? That person must have played the sport. I think if a person sets an example by his or her performance, it's the most convincing thing that person can do. No one can say, "Well, how do you know? You've never done it yourself. Why should I follow your advice?" If you've done it yourself, that's the most convincing thing there is. People will not imitate anyone they do not admire. Learning is following in the footsteps of another individual.

Great speakers are not afraid of overcoming obstacles . . . to them, obstacles are more or less a challenge. They are not afraid of doing whatever it takes, and they will not be defeated by obstacles. They speak from their heart, they know what they're talking about, they've done it, and they believe in what they are saying. So many times, I'll see a speaker get up who possesses in-depth academic knowledge and is correct in it, but unless that person has done it him- or herself, the words don't write themselves indelibly in my mind.

Then there are people who have brilliant ideas and have lived them, and you may follow their ideas. But for some reason, they "walk from the bright room to the dark room" . . . they venture too close to the dark side of human nature. You may admire and even follow their ideas, but you may not admire them as people. If you get to the place where you don't admire the individual, it's a struggle to hang on to those ideas.

Now, I admired Dr. Peale so much as a man, and his principles are associated with him as a person. I'll never be able to divorce the ideas from the man. That's one of the reasons he was so great — he was great as a man. Certain principles are so much stronger if you can associate them with an individual.

Likewise, wonderful ideas are like products, and you lose so much if you get to the point where you no longer associate them with their sources . . . they become mere words you could read in a book. But if you associate them with an individual, you cling to them and are more loyal to those principles, because you think, "I want to be like that person."

There isn't any force in the world as strong as the feeling that "he . . . or she . . . believes in me." It's the same as associating an idea or principle with its source . . . the individual. If you know that a person believes in you and that person is a mentor, it's the most powerful thing in the world. If you get to the point where you lose the relationship of the mentor — that person believing in you and you believing in them — you lose so much.

Creative expectancy is so much more powerful than self-fulfilling prophecy. It's so powerful letting someone know you believe in them: "I know you can do it . . . sure, you can do it!" Yes, it's helpful to put a picture on your wall of whatever you want and to say, "I know I'm going to get that car . . . I know I can do it," and that is self-fulfilling prophecy. But with creative expectancy, someone believing in you . . . there is nothing more powerful than that. Why do you think a child learns to walk, even though it may fall down 500,000 times trying? Creative expectancy . . . the mother or father saying, when the child falls down, "Come on, honey . . . get up! I know you can do it . . . I know you can walk! Come on, come on . . . I *know* you can do it!"

But as an adult, you've got to feel the other person really believes in you, not just brags on you. You don't want to be thinking, "Oh, don't give me that stuff . . . I've heard that before." But if you *know* they believe in you, it's a relationship, not just advice . . . it's a powerful relationship.

HAVE YOU EVER SPOKEN TO A U.S. PRESIDENT?

One of the congressmen invited me to speak to a joint session of the Senate and the House in Washington. It was a small meeting, kind of a routine thing. They asked me to submit my speech in writing, and they entered it into the congressional record.

Another incident was when I was invited to a friend's house, and Ronald Reagan's father-in-law, Dr. Loyal Davis — who was president of the American Neurosurgical Association and a prominent doctor — was invited. Ronald Reagan was there, too, and I met him . . . this was when he was governor of California. He was a very personable fellow, and he stated that he would someday be running for national office.

WHAT IS YOUR MOST MEMORABLE SPEECH?

The most memorable speech I ever made was when I was on the same program with Dr. Norman Vincent Peale. John Hammond set it up where Dr. Peale, Paul Harvey, Art Linkletter and I were on the program. They called them "rallies" — this one was in Atlanta, Georgia, as I recall — and we each spoke about 30 minutes. I was so excited that I was on the program with these wonderful people! I was so inspired listening to them . . . you could see they were speaking from their hearts . . . and I got swept up in the whole feeling. It wasn't just an academic thing. I felt humble and grateful that I had this opportunity. I remember I was the next to the last one on the program, and I was trying so hard to give something from my heart . . . some "do-how" instead of just "know-how."

Another memorable time was when I was trying to get Dr. Peale to come speak to our NSA meeting in New Orleans, and Ruth Peale helped to convince him to change his schedule and speak for us. It wasn't exactly a "speech" . . . the "audience" consisted of only two people, Ruth Peale and Dr. Peale . . . but it was probably the most important presentation in my life. It helped to change the course of history for the National Speakers Association.

THE
NATIONAL SPEAKERS ASSOCIATION

HOW DID THE NATIONAL SPEAKERS ASSOCIATION BEGIN?

In about 1966, I started really exploring the possibilities of speaking and holding seminars around the country for a fee, and I found some very startling facts. First, as near as I could determine, about 90 percent of the meeting planners used doctors as speakers, 7 percent of the planners used lawyers, but — from the information I could gather — only about 3 percent of the companies and conventions ever used paid speakers outside of the organization.

Except for those few professional speakers, most were politicians. Frankly, they were more interested in getting votes than in giving helpful ideas or information. And, of course, there were a few ol' retired cronies from the organization itself. So the quality of the speakers wasn't too good.

I remember asking certain program chairs why they didn't have more outside speakers. Basically, they'd give the same answer: "Well, we had one of those so-called professional speakers years ago . . . never again!" Now, I'm not saying there weren't some great speakers around, because there were . . . but they were rare.

At that time, there was this problem of transportation. For instance, Red Motley — the originator of the expression, "Nothing happens until someone sells something" — observed that speakers had to travel by train; jet travel was just not available to most speakers on the circuit. He said that even if a person went on the circuit full time, they would be lucky to get in more than two or three speeches a week unless the engagements could be arranged in the same area. It's interesting to note that the convention planner always seems to pick the speaker who lives farthest from the convention site!

Many people wanted to become professional speakers but just didn't know how to start. Sure, we had our Toastmasters clubs, Dale Carnegie courses . . . even college courses in public speaking. But helpful as they were, none of these could tell people how to develop the type of speech that people were willing to pay for. Also, none of them could tell people how to secure speaking engagements for a fee.

During the first few years after a person starts speaking for a fee, at least 80 to 90 percent of his or her energies must be directed toward marketing that talent. A person can be a fantastic speaker and yet remain one of the best-kept secrets in America. While speakers must be careful not to go on the circuit until they are ready . . . because one appearance can be overexposure if they are *not* ready . . . when speakers are ready, they must pursue a well-organized plan of marketing.

So, at that time, there was nowhere to go to learn all the facets of becoming a professional speaker. If a person wanted to become a doctor, that person, if he were fortunate enough, could enter medical school. If a person wanted to follow the profession of law, we had our law schools. But not so in professional speaking. There was no place to go to learn all the necessary ingredients of making a professional income in the field of speaking.

I remember one of the first things I did was to write the few booking agents in existence at that time. Practically all of them were concentrating on entertainers in the field and not on speakers. Those who showed any interest were only interested in the very few speakers who were already popular . . . and they didn't need the bookings! So, getting an agent was certainly not the answer for a new person desiring to enter the field of paid speaking — or at least not the means to a livelihood.

During my first year as a professional speaker, I was only charging $150 per speech or seminar, and it was costing me about $250 to secure each speech. The next year, I charged $250 per speech, but the percentage of profit was practically no better. This pattern of spending more than I took in was a stupid approach, but there was no precedent to follow . . . no one to look to for help. I realized that only about a tenth of what I was doing to get bookings was bringing any results, but since I couldn't discover which tenth it was, I kept wasting money over the first two years.

About that time, Merlyn Cundiff and I became associated in conducting seminars. She had also become frustrated in her initial approach to the speaking field, so we decided it would be a good idea to invite a group of speakers together for several days in order that each could profit from the ideas of the others. We called it the Phoenix Summer Sales Seminar, and our first meeting was held in 1969 at the Camelback Inn in Phoenix, Arizona.

Although only about 35 people attended the first meeting, so enthusiastic were those who attended, and so profitable were the results from the exchange of ideas, that the seminar was repeated each year. Over 70 attended the second year, and over 100 the third and fourth years.

Not only did the "old pros" begin attending, but those who wanted to enter the profession came to profit from the generous sharing of ideas. Training programs designed to protect the newcomers from the expensive mistakes experienced by many of us were set up. In all promotional materials, two things were emphasized above everything else. First: Speaking, to be a profession, must be participated in by professionals. Second: The only way to become a professional is through OPE — other people's experience.

Mark Twain said it best: "If a cat sits on a hot stove once, it'll never sit on a hot stove again . . . but it'll never sit on a cold one, either. It gets out of the business of sitting on stoves!" Many of us had learned the hard and expensive way, through trial and error, which was foolish. No truer statement was ever made than, "The only thing worth more secondhand than firsthand is experience!" and it certainly applies in every respect to speaking.

This was really the background and gestation period of the birth of our National Speakers Association. About two years before NSA was incorporated, speakers at the Phoenix Summer Sales Seminar began asking why an organization similar to the American Medical Association, for doctors, or the American Bar Association, for lawyers, couldn't be created for speakers. So, the interest was there. Still, NSA's first year was very discouraging. We sent out at least four mailings to all speakers whose names and addresses could be discovered. While a few recipients of the mailings embraced the concept from the very beginning, most of the initial answers were very discouraging: "Oh, it's been tried before . . . it'll never work!" "Who's trying to capitalize on the organization?" "Is it to be used by a few to get more speaking engagements?" "If it survives for a year, I might be interested in joining." "I won't join until I know who's on the board of directors."

After that year of discouragement and very little positive response, it became apparent what we should have known from the beginning: that developing a speakers association was a real selling job! Most of it had to be done in person. In designing a new set of purposes, which we worked on the second year . . . a whole year from the incorporation . . . we realized that several things were necessary if we ever would be able to secure a nucleus for incorporation.

First, the purposes of the National Speakers Association must be carefully explained to all prospective members. Prospects were to be assured that NSA's prime purpose was to promote the high ethical and professional standards of the association's members. To this end, training seminars would be conducted periodically for NSA members.

Second, in no way was NSA to be used by any group to secure speaking engagements. It would never be permitted to exist for the selfish interests of a few. It was hoped, however, that the public would recognize a member of NSA as one who adhered to the high standards of the profession.

Finally, all promotional materials would assure prospective members that quality of membership would not be sacrificed for numbers. During the second year of contacting speakers regarding the possibility of organizing a national speakers association, a little different approach was made in the many communications sent out from our office.

By this time, Merlyn and I had an office with a part-time secretary to assist with promotions. Everyone contacted was asked for ideas, suggestions and recommendations for possible members. The letters even asked for suggestions as to an initial board of directors and suggested officers for the first year. After approximately two years of contacting speakers, we felt that we had commitments from enough of them to risk incorporation and an initial start.

Consequently, Merlyn and I went to the office of Sid Rosen, an attorney in Phoenix who had shown interest in becoming a member. He agreed to incorporate and represent the association without a fee, which was a most generous gesture. As the organization's attorney, Sid asked Merlyn and me to be the two incorporators in the group's initial articles of incorporation on July 12, 1973.

The people who attended the first board meetings were Chris Hegarty, Dr. Cody Sweet, Don Hutson, Ken Lewis, Joe Larson, Bill Gove, Dr. Carl Winters, John Hammond, Merlyn and me. In the minutes of the first meeting, where we elected the association's first officers, we were very careful to suggest the names of potential officers who had been recommended in numerous letters from prospective members.

The first NSA president was Bill Gove . . . everyone wanted Bill Gove. They also suggested Dr. Carl Winters, who became our first vice president; Don Hutson, our second vice president; and Merlyn, our first secretary-treasurer. I decided never to hold an NSA office so there would be no question as to any self-serving purposes in regard to my work with the organization.

A group of speakers living in Phoenix and known as Platform Professionals, about 20 in number, joined almost unanimously the day of our incorporation. I believe that gave us kind of an impetus in beginning the National Speakers Association.

The Phoenix Summer Sales Seminar was held for two years in Phoenix even after NSA was incorporated. We held it two days prior to our NSA meetings at the Camelback Inn. Practically the same speakers attended both. Very soon, it became apparent that NSA was becoming a healthy organization, growing in every respect, and there was really no danger that it would not take the same role for speakers that the American Bar Association had taken for lawyers or the American Medical Association had taken for doctors. All officers on the original board of directors named in the NSA articles of incorporation had attended and been supporters of the Phoenix Summer Sales Seminar, and practically everyone who had attended our Phoenix Summer Sales Seminar had joined NSA.

Merlyn and I had a lot of sentiment about the Phoenix Summer Sales Seminar after holding it for eight years, but we knew that it had served its purpose. Consequently, we contacted those who were constant attendees, told them that the seminar would be held no longer and urged those who had not already joined NSA to do so. Fortunately, most of them did . . . and in a nutshell, that's the story of the Phoenix Summer Sales Seminar. Dead but not forgotten, it had served its purpose.

In spite of the interest in speaking as a profession and in NSA as an organization, there still were very few speakers who were getting out and making any money speaking. As I've said, paid speaking was done mainly by retired executives, movie people, politicians and so forth. But when people started seeing that speaking could be a profession and that you could get paid for it if you were good enough, many of them decided they would learn to make money by speaking. It was amazing how many people came together! We would have seminars where we would teach people not only to be better salespeople but also to be professional teachers of other people — not only professional speakers, but also professional trainers. That's when the thing really started.

I remember Dr. Peale saying, "Cavett, this has been tried twice. The first time, it got up to about 15 people, and the people wanted to profit by it, so they cut off the membership. It was tried again, and they again closed off the membership at a certain point to discourage competition. Cavett, there is a need for this organization. There isn't anything that can't be accomplished when the right people are swept up in a worthy cause, divorced from who gets credit for what. As long as the main purpose is to help people and train people, it will go, because there is a need for this kind of thing."

I said, "Dr. Peale, you've certainly helped a lot," and he said, "Cavett, I want to continue to help, and if you will stay with it and work with it, I promise I will back you up." From that moment on, I decided I would never be an officer of NSA.

54

I remember one year, it looked like we weren't going to have enough money to be able to go through the year because Meryln and I were putting up most of the money ourselves. I was very discouraged, and I thought, "If I could ever get Dr. Peale to come and speak at our national convention and advertise it, I could get a lot of new members." So I contacted Dr. Peale . . . I was speaking in New York at the time . . . and I sat with him in his office, in the presence of Ruth, his wife. I said, "Dr. Peale, we need you so much. I don't know if we can make it another year. We haven't got any money to pay you, but could you be the principal speaker at our national convention in New Orleans?"

Dr. Peale replied, "I'm sorry, Cavett, but I've got an engagement in China and can't do it" I'll never forget how Ruth Spoke up and said, "Now, wait a minute, Norman. I hear you say that if Cavett worked on this thing and got it going for a few years, you'd stand behind him. He needs you very much now, and you know you can change the date of your China engagement. you are going to accept that invitation!" She really said that! Later on, Dr. Peale and I laughed about it, and we've talked about it many times since.

So, Dr. Peale spoke at the New Orleans convention when we most needed it. We really did a lot of advertising, and we had over 300 people attend that convention . . . more than three times the number of people who'd ever attended NSA's national convention! People came from all over the country. Dr. Peale made one of the most dynamic speeches ever made on how we could build the organization, how much this profession was needed and how the NSA was as necessary as the American Bar Association or the American Medical Association. He said we can all make this happen if we all stand behind it. That was the greatest thing that ever happened to NSA . . . that gave the organization the strength it's still feeling.

HOW DID THE NATIONAL SPEAKERS ASSOCIATION GROW?

■   ■   ■

In the beginning, all we knew — because we had no precedent to follow — was that some of us wanted to make a living from speaking. Our original thinking was that we would restrict membership to those who wanted to learn to be professional speakers. All of a sudden, we had people coming in and saying things like, "Look . . . I've just been elected president of the Underwriters Association of California. I don't want to go into speaking professionally, but I want to learn how to be a good speaker for the kinds of presentations I'll be doing." Others came in saying, "I'm a training director, and I want to know how to communicate to my trainees." We found very soon that there was a larger concept to this thing.

A lot of people who were entertainers wanted to join us, saying, "I want to build a better rapport with my audience." People who could provide services to the meetings industry — such as bureaus and suppliers — said, "We can customize our services just for the meetings industry." So very soon, we realized that NSA had a larger purpose to fulfill . . . and that's why we welcomed entertainers as well as sales managers and business executives.

Then there are the people whose jobs depended on bringing in good speakers. I had people call and say, "If I get in a poor speaker, I've really jeopardized my job. I'd like to know where I can go to hear good speakers." So, we got a lot of members who came in to look speakers over — which, of course, is good for the speakers, too. So, NSA opened itself up to anyone interested in the professionalization of the meetings industry.

During Dr. Carl Winters' NSA presidency, the association's growth and membership started increasing. Merlyn and I sat down and talked about who would be the best executive director for NSA, because we could no longer handle that position ourselves. After asking around for ideas on capable people, we came up with the same individual: Bill Johnson. On a Sunday morning, Merlyn made a long-distance call to Bill, who was in Tucson that day. She said, "Bill, we've got a problem, and we need your help!" He was eager to help and within minutes became our executive director.

It's been a long time since the idea for the National Speakers Association originated. I hesitate to mention the names of those involved, because there were so many dedicated speakers who wanted to see the dream realized. People like Bob Bale, Charlie Cullen and others who are no longer with us helped in many respects. The great Red Motley — former chairman of the board of *Parade Magazine* and first honorary member of NSA, as voted by the NSA board — did his share.

Dr. Peale often said that the first ingredient of a successful project is that the project is divorced from who gets credit for what, and that's been one of the fine things about NSA. The association's first six presidents — Bill Gove, Carl Winters, Don Hutson, Joe Larson, Ira Hayes and Ty Boyd — as well as all subsequent NSA presidents have worked diligently and with complete dedication, putting personal gain aside for the growth and welfare of our great NSA. Also, our board of directors has been just as interested, energetic and dedicated.

One great accomplishment of NSA is this: Years ago, there was a feeling that only a certain number of speeches and seminars could be made each year at conventions . . . the pie was just so big. Anytime a speaker secured an engagement, it cut down the number of remaining slices for other speakers. But NSA has increased the size of the pie. Every time a presenter does a good job, he or she increases the size of the pie.

As I said earlier, it used to be that only 3 percent of conventions featured outside speakers. I'm confident that number is accurate. But thanks to NSA and the fine professional speakers it has both produced and attracted, that percentage has been raised considerably. We have a long way to go, but NSA is working on it . . . and we ain't through yet!

I always try to convey to new NSA members that if they have half the opportunities we had to observe the hard work and dedication of so many people over the years, they will be just as proud as we are to be members of our great professional association.

It's so amazing to see the progress of some of the association's young speakers. I remember new people showing up who, as Bill Gove would say, "couldn't lead a group in silent prayer," and they would make it to the top of the profession! And I'm so pleased that the older, more mature speakers are so willing to help the young speakers.

I remember the time one of the young speakers came to his first meeting . . . I think it was Keith DeGreen or Mark Hansen. He said to me later, "I couldn't believe it! Charlie Jarvis stayed up until 3 in the morning helping me . . . and he acted as though he enjoyed it!" Knowing Charlie, I'm sure he did. He's a true pro and willing to give unselfishly.

I think the difference between a real artist and just an entertaining speaker is the dedication some of these pros, like ol' Bob Bale and Ken McFarland, showed to their profession. I believe, from the bottom of my heart, that a person is not a real pro unless he feels an obligation to his profession, including the desire to be replaced by someone even better than he is. When I say that, I mean that a person wants to replace *her*self by someone better than *she* is, too! I believe we all must spend time with and show dedication to the younger speakers, not expecting anything in return.

I'll tell you what gets my goat, though . . . these telephone calls I get from people all over the United States, saying, "Well, my business is shot, I'm facing bankruptcy, and I'm tired of it. I see you guys having a lot of fun traveling around the country . . . eating a lot of good food and so forth, and I just want to chuck it all and go on the circuit. How do I get started?" What I'd *like* to say is, "Get down on your bended knees and pray for a little common sense!" What I usually say is, "Every day of your life, listen to at least two to three hours' worth of speaking-oriented audiotapes!"

I remember some time ago, I did a program in Texas. I'd just finished a three-hour seminar, and a young attorney came up to me and said, "You're absolutely phenomenal! I sat there and listened to you speak, and I thought, 'My God, he must have practiced that speech all week!'" Of course, I'd been practicing for at least 10 years!

The moral of the story for people coming into the profession is this: Speaking is not something you explode into, it's something you grow into. It's not something you decide today or tomorrow — "I'm going to be a speaker" — it's something you dedicate your whole life to. It's not a profession, it's a way of living.

Carl Winters had some beautiful beliefs, and one of my favorites is: "If you want to be a real pro, you've got to have a message within you that's crying for expression . . . one that will not stay inside — a real message that rides on the wings of humor to make it digestible and that's delivered with a few stories to remember it by." I think that's a beautiful statement.

I remember a time Merlyn and I were speaking, I think it was in Indianapolis, and someone came up and said to me, "You know, I'd like to go on the circuit. Do you have to be funny in order to be a public speaker?" I remembered something the great Bill Gove said, and replied, "No . . . only if you want to be paid!"

HOW DID **NSA** MATURE?

Two of the most exciting things that evolved in NSA were the fantastic Council of Peers Award of Excellence (CPAE) and the Certified Speaking Professional (CSP) award. Bringing a new dimension to the organization, these coveted awards signify their recipients' high level of professionalism. Like everything in NSA, I guess, these awards fell on hard times at the start. Because they are misunderstood by some, I encourage people to read about them in detail in NSA brochures. They aren't about patting your fellow speakers on the back. They're really very tough awards to earn — somewhat like the CLU in life insurance, the CAE for association executives or the GRI in real estate. These are very prestigious awards, and I'm excited about their growth. I hope they will be great tools for inspiring young speakers to reach the pinnacle of their potential.

Achieving excellence in public speaking is not an overnight proposition. We've got instant coffee and instant tea, but there's no "quickie" solution when it comes to human development. You don't throw an egg into the barnyard and expect it to crow tomorrow. Proficiency has to be earned and not just learned . . . then you appreciate it more. I think a career in speaking is finally being viewed as a real challenge, with people realizing that you must study to be a speaker, just as you would for any other profession.

NSA provides great educational opportunities for those who want to learn. I'm very encouraged by our monthly magazine and our audio magazine, both of which provide material readers can actually apply and use. Our winter workshops and national conventions are getting better every year, and our wonderful international center will help NSA grow into the new millennium and the high-tech, global aspect of communications. The specialized laboratories held there are intimate learning experiences geared toward specific competencies and offering very individualized attention.

Since 1979, NSA has honored me by presenting the Cavett Award to one NSA member each year. Although some call it "the Oscar of professional speaking," I am more proud of the fact that it's given to the NSA member who best exemplifies the qualities of caring, sharing, loving and making a difference in people's lives. I hope that I have lived up to those principles.

NSA is a different organization today than it was years ago, and that's just as it should be: keeping pace with changing times. One thing I hope will never change, though, is the caring-sharing, loving-hugging attitude of its members toward those who want to improve themselves. We now have a real profession . . . let's keep it that way!

57

WHAT DOES IT FEEL LIKE TO BE THE FOUNDER OF **NSA,** LOOKING OUT ON ALL THOSE PEOPLE?

I think the organization would have formed anyway, but I was fortunate enough, and had the privilege of being in a situation, where I just kind of opened the doors, and the genius flowed through from so many people who wanted to help.

The National Speakers Association was not formed by any one, two or half-dozen people. It was a group of people who got the concept and figured there was a need for it . . . a need for people to come together and exchange ideas on how we can help people become speakers. But we can do something even greater than that . . . we can help people qualify themselves to go out and help other people live better lives. NSA did more for me than I can ever pay back. It changed my life so much . . . I began believing in the things I was teaching.

It has an eternal, lasting influence when you teach people to speak. And even more so when you teach them to teach *others* to speak. And those teach others, and they teach others, and it spreads like a prairie fire on a windy day . . . it just spreads in all directions.

It would give me a great deal of joy when people wrote me and said, "I took those principles from your speech, and they worked. I've taught them to other people, and they changed their lives." There isn't anything more powerful than teaching people to live more abundantly. When I look out on all those people at an NSA convention, I feel so blessed I've had the joy of feeling that maybe I made a difference in other people's lives. Dr. Peale made a difference in my life, and I figured I owed it to the public to make a difference in other people's lives . . . that's the way I pay back. When people do something great for you, the way to repay them is to follow their example and do something great for someone else and pass it on . . . pass it on.

FAMILY LIFE:
TRUDY AND THE KIDS

HOW DID YOU MEET YOUR WIFE, TRUDY?

In my second year of law school, a friend of mine had a picture of a beautiful girl in his room. I saw it and asked if he could introduce me to her. Her name was Bobbie Bennett, and she went to Sweet Briar College. My friend wrote her, and Bobbie wrote me back and said she'd give me a date. In those days, people didn't go steady . . . the more dates you had, the better. There were cars going over to Sweet Briar College all the time, and I'd catch a ride with them.

Lexington, Virginia, was where Washington and Lee University was, and 40 miles away was Lynchburg, near Sweet Briar College. Every weekend, the boys from W&L, VMI and the University of Virginia would drive to Sweet Briar and the other women's colleges to have dates. I used to work all week to find a ride there. For $2, you could take the bus over to Lynchburg.

So, I went to Sweet Briar to meet Bobbie. I remember it so well . . . I called on her, and she came down the stairs with Trudy walking beside her. Bobbie said that her boyfriend from the University of Virginia had shown up, so she had arranged a blind date for me with Trudy.

Of course, Trudy was almost as pretty then as she is now. She had been Miss South Carolina of 1929, and I went nuts over her! I hadn't had a date with anyone for a long time. When I found out she was the daughter of the man who had taught me chemistry at Furman University, and then remembered she was the little girl who had pushed me into the pool when I worked as a lifesaver at the Furman pool, I fell in love with her.

I remember way back when Dr. Buist, Trudy's father, taught me chemistry. He used to have about six or seven of us students over for dinner and tell us that if we passed our chemistry exam, we could have a date with one of his three daughters. Trudy will swear this is not true . . . that her parents used to have some of the faculty members over but that her mother was teaching then and didn't have time to feed six or seven boys on the weekends. Trudy says, "I think you have told this story so often that you believe it yourself!"

I saw Trudy on the weekends, and Sis would invite her over to the dances at W&L. When they visited, Trudy and her roommate, Bobbie, would stay at the university president's home, where I was living with Brother and Sis. That was the only way I had enough prestige that Trudy would say, "Yes, I'll come over!"

One spring holiday, I caught a ride and went down to visit Trudy. Her parents had arranged for me to stay at the home of their cousins, the Hollises, who were away on vacation at the time. I remember the first night I was there, I was so thrilled — and I was a hell of a jokester . . . crazy — that I called up and told Trudy's mother, "I'm in real trouble, here. I'm at the Hollises' house, and the police saw the light on and have arrested me for breaking into the house!" Trudy's mother said, "Here . . . speak to Dr. Buist," and I told him the same thing, and he said, "What in the blazes! Let me speak to them!" Then I said, "Wait, I was just joking with you," and he just blew up and said, "Well, that's a devil of a joke . . . to call and pull a thing like that." I was scared to go there the next day, and I apologized so profusely about it. That was a heck of a way to start a relationship with Trudy's parents, but they were so sweet to me and forgave me for it.

After Trudy finished at Sweet Briar, I still had another year left of law school. Trudy went home to Greenville, South Carolina, while I finished, and she wrote me every day. She was a talented and clever artist and drew pictures all over the envelopes. We saved those letters with the artwork for many years until a flood in our garage destroyed them.

The summer after graduating from W&L, I went down to Columbus, Mississippi, where Mother was staying with her Aunt Connor. My brother Joe and Evelyn had just married and were about to leave on their honeymoon. They were going up to Richmond and were going by Greenville, and I just demanded that they let me catch a ride with them to Greenville to visit Trudy. I remember they were so mad about it, but Mother thought they should do it. There was quite a to-do about it, but they finally let me join them. I remember they would hardly speak to me. We stopped somewhere overnight, and I slept in the car.

TELL US ABOUT YOUR CHILDREN.

When our kids were growing up, things were very different. Child rearing was considered Trudy's domain, and bringing in the money was considered my department. There were very few dual-income families back then. I felt a tremendous sense of responsibility to pass the bar exam so I could make an income for the family.

60

Once a week, we had "family night," when we would go out for Mexican food, or sometimes I would go downtown and get hot caramel corn and we'd all watch a movie on TV.

I used to take a lot of pleasure in going hunting and fishing with my two sons, and going to tennis tournaments with them. I felt that those things were important in my own upbringing, so I wanted to give the boys the same pleasures I had experienced.

JoAnn

When our first child, JoAnn, was born, I was in Tucson, Arizona, taking the bar exam. JoAnn came a little early . . . we weren't expecting her to arrive while I was in Tucson. My nephew, who was living with us at the time, took Trudy to the hospital.

When JoAnn was a little girl, she was very beautiful and very philosophical, in a childlike way. She would sit and contemplate and then say, "I hope I have a good life." I always thought that was a strange thing for a little girl to say, and nothing seemed to prompt her to say it. It was almost like she had a premonition that she would have a life different from other people's.

JoAnn grew into a beautiful young woman with a great deal of ambition. She had a lot of recognition at school as a beauty queen and pom-pom girl. She was very popular and went out on a lot of dates. After she finished school, she went to San Francisco, then New York, to pursue a modeling career.

In New York, JoAnn began to have some serious health problems. We had her go to Payne-Whitney Hospital in New York City to have her examined, and the doctor diagnosed her as paranoid-schizophrenic. They said she would be in and out of hospitals for the rest of her life. JoAnn stayed at the hospital in New York City for over a year. It was a tremendous blow to Trudy and me. In fact, Trudy had to be hospitalized herself at the time of JoAnn's diagnosis, she was so devastated.

The extraordinary thing about JoAnn was that she functioned relatively well compared to many other people with her disease. She married and had two children. Every few years, she would become "destabilized" and need to be hospitalized for a few weeks at a time. Then she would regain her emotional stability. She was a very loving mother.

At age 50, JoAnn became destabilized and never did regain her mental stability. Eventually, she lived in a supervised-care home. One day, she wandered away from the group home and didn't return. The police were notified, and several days later, her body was found. Her life had been taken by two young gang members, the younger of whom was only 14 years old. It was a very sad time for our whole family.

We had a most beautiful memorial service for JoAnn, and it was something that brought a lot of strength to the family when we all saw how much love and sweetness she had brought into our lives. Her two boys, William Cavett Saacke and Robert Carter Saacke, got up at the service and spoke about how much they loved her and how she never showed anything but love and affection for them. The service affirmed how much she had meant in the lives of others, and it took away some of the pain we felt.

Cavett Jr.

My elder son, Cavett Jr., was very athletic as a boy and eventually became quite good at tennis. He went to the University of Pennsylvania Medical School and became a neurosurgeon. Cavett Jr. was always a high achiever and kept his athletics going. He became a triathlete and participated in the Iron Man in his 50s. He married a beautiful and talented woman whose name is Sande. She is a very talented artist and gardener, and they have two little girls named Wesley Anne and Ashley Cavett.

Cavett Jr. has been a high achiever at everything he ever set his mind to. He is very knowledgeable about the computer. He not only has been a presenter at several American Medical Association meetings, he eventually was elected president of the California Neurosurgical Association.

61

'Wicky'

My younger son, Bill — the family calls him "Wicky," short for William — has many exceptional gifts and talents. In his high school years, his SAT scores were in the upper two percentile in the nation. He had a flair for mathematics, philosophy and religion, sports, drama and music, too. He went to Princeton University and graduated in three-and-a-half years in philosophy and religion. He also was in the glee club and on the rugby team.

The family felt that Bill made some unusual decisions — like quitting Princeton after his second year to join a monastery. This appeared to be a highly unusual decision for him, but we wanted to be supportive. Trudy cried, but we just felt he was the kind of person who perhaps "marched to the beat of his own drummer." As time went on, however, the monastic life proved not to be a harmonious choice for Bill, and he came home. The next year, he went back to Princeton to finish his studies.

Because we'd had some experience with mental illness in the family, we soon started identifying the signs in Bill. Early in his adult life, he, too, was diagnosed with schizophrenia. To begin with, both JoAnn and Wicky had episodes of mental illness, then would be completely normal for two years. Then it would hit again. This pattern was a two-edged sword — in some ways, it gave us time as a family to get used to the condition a little at a time . . . but in other ways, it made it harder, because you could never quite adjust one way or the other.

When it became apparent that Wicky had the disease, too, it was especially hard for the family to take. We knew what to expect, and it seemed incomprehensible that another of our family was afflicted. But modern medicine is constantly improving the medications that can help control the symptoms.

Since I retired, Trudy and I have been able to go to lunch with Wicky and his life partner, Ingrid, on a weekly basis. I've come to realize that the benchmarks of success are different for everyone. It used to be that I had ambitions for Wicky to become a teacher or a speaker or a preacher, and I used to measure his actions against how close he came to those ideals.

But when I began to realize that Wicky had a different road ahead of him, I could appreciate his other successes — creating a loving home for himself, taking care of Ingrid and sharing loving moments with family. I am now better able to appreciate his unique gifts to me in my life. Bill's illness has not affected his ability to love people at all, and he is a very sweet and loving person.

The Twins: Lee and Lyn

Lee and Lyn, our twins, were so tiny when they were born, they could fit in a little bowl on the dinner table . . . or right in the palms of my hands! I was so afraid they weren't going to live, but a good friend who was a doctor came to visit us after they were born and said that God gives babies more of what they need to fight to live than we have even as adults.

Sure enough, the twins did make it and have been a great blessing to Trudy and me, especially as we've gotten older. They helped us move out of the home we lived in as a family for almost 50 years. We couldn't have done it without them. We are fortunate enough to see them every week.

The twins also helped Trudy and me adjust to the best course of action to take with Wicky when his illness was diagnosed. Lyn was working with me when Trudy and I were trying to take care of Wicky at our home. We'd almost turned the house into a hospital, and it was a very stressful environment for all of us. We didn't realize he could get the help he needed elsewhere.

We also didn't know we were eligible for financial assistance from the federal government to manage Wicky's care. This is a common misconception, and we spent hundreds of thousands of dollars over many years on hospitals and medical treatment. As adults, both Wicky and JoAnn were eligible for county and federal aid, but it took some investigative work to find this out. It was Lyn who said to us, "We've got to get some help."

Lyn called the county health department and asked what we could do. It was very discouraging, because the laws were such that you had to prove that a person was a danger to himself or someone else before you could get help for him. After many, many dramatic incidents and hospitalizations, Wicky finally built up enough of a record that it was not as difficult to get help for him. Around that time, Lyn wanted to pursue a career in teaching and stopped working at my business to do so.

Lee came to work with me before I retired. She moved back to Phoenix from San Francisco, where she had earned her living as a professional singer and entertainer for many years. She sang at the Fairmont Hotel and the Marc Hopkins Hotel with large orchestras. She also taught and had her own business selling and performing entertainment services in Northern California. Lee is experienced in sales and marketing, and I asked her to come work with me in the family business. As a talented performer and businesswoman in her own right, she is carrying on with our speaking/consulting business as president of Cavett Robert Communications. We go to Toastmasters and NSA meetings regularly when she is in town.

In the early '90s, Lee wrote the following essay describing some of the experiences we've had over the years adjusting to our family's special health challenges. I hope it may be helpful to other families.

A SPECIAL CHRISTMAS GIFT

On Christmas Eve, my family had a very special experience.

My brother Wicky (a nickname for William) was diagnosed in early adulthood with a disease called schizophrenia. Schizophrenia is a chronic mental illness that affects the brain's chemistry and circuitry. It takes a great deal of skill to take care of someone with a chronic illness, and many people live in a supervised home to get the support they need to function outside of a hospital environment.

My parents took care of Wicky for a long time, but with much counseling and family support, they agreed to let go and allow another option to develop to give my brother the support he needed.

When our family first tried to guide my brother into a more appropriate living situation, he ran away. It must be very difficult to face a chronic illness, and Wicky was in denial for a while. He was homeless for some time, and we did not know where he was. It was very painful. We learned a lot about the homeless then — for example, over 50 percent of the homeless are chronically mentally ill individuals who have "slipped through the cracks."

After his experience with homelessness, Wicky started getting behind his treatment program and taking his medications. He went through many not-so-good supervised-care homes and medications before we were able to help him find the ones that gave him the most support to live an active life. Families often experience great emotional trauma watching their loved ones move in and out of the less-than-perfect mental health system.

At one point, my brother's doctor called me and said that Wicky was eligible to be a trial patient for a new "miracle" drug for schizophrenia called clozapine. The white blood count of those taking this medication must be monitored, so it's an expensive drug to take. Plus, the government health program called AHCESS has a waiting list for this drug. (Later, Wicky took part in a trial for another new drug for controlling schizophrenia, risperidon.)

Wicky began the clozapine program, and after an initial period of destabilization, some remarkable results started taking place. My brother called me and said, "I can remember things that I couldn't remember before . . . things about growing up with the family."

For Christmas that year, he asked my parents for a new jacket and shirt. This in itself was a miracle. I never thought I'd ever again see my brother in a nice jacket during my lifetime. Self-care is a beautiful expression of human dignity, and Wicky's improved dramatically with his treatment.

On Christmas Eve, Wicky came to dinner wearing a handsome jacket and turtleneck sweater. His clothes looked clean, his hair was clean and cut, he was shaven, and the dimples in his cheeks reappeared. My brother even displayed his famous sense of humor and wit. For a long time, this man — a Princeton graduate, a member of the elite intellectual club called MENSA and the author of two books on philosophy and religion . . . quite a brilliant young man — had not seemed to want to communicate with anyone but the voices he heard in his head. But this night, he joined in the conversation in a delightful way! Humor is a great indicator of mental health.

When we exchanged presents that evening, Wicky was so excited giving his gifts to everyone that he squirmed like a child. It takes a lot of mental health to enjoy giving — it means you are not self-absorbed but have evolved outside of yourself to enjoy thinking about other people's happiness.

My brother gave us a wonderful gift that Christmas. He taught us that the dignity of the human spirit, good humor and the expansiveness to share with those you love are the greatest gifts we can give each other. I felt a hope reborn. Maybe this was truly the gift of the baby Jesus in the Christmas story: that the possibility of hope for the new year can be reborn in this lifetime if we are open to receiving it and sharing it with others.

HOW DID YOU COPE WITH THE TIME AWAY FROM YOUR CHILDREN WHEN YOU STARTED TRAVELING SO MUCH, AND DO YOU THINK IT AFFECTED THEM?

I think whether you are a doctor, a lawyer or a preacher, a teacher or a plumber, if you have a family, you must give great consideration to balancing your time. How much time must you spend with your family, and what amount of time must you spend going out to make a living? So many people will make excuses for neglecting their family . . . they'll go around having a lot of fun and excuse themselves by saying, "I'm doing it for my family" or "I have to go out and build a clientele" or "I have to get experience" or "I'm doing this because I love my family so much." I, too, have been guilty of that. Taking that attitude is a temptation.

When I started speaking, for the first time in my life, I started taking joy in my work. I'd never taken real joy in my work as a lawyer, but when I started speaking, I just loved doing it so much. I took such joy in it that sometimes, I'll admit, I went on the road too much.

I believe that life is so scheduled that a person can balance the two and work hard to not let career interfere with family life. A person seems to have a greater stimulus and a greater spiritual ambition if he or she does not neglect family. You learn certain things with your family that you can use and apply and relate to certain principles in business. There are some things to be learned from your family that you cannot learn anywhere else.

When I started in the profession of speaking, I didn't have any role models. When I was busy speaking, I was away from home 12 or 15 days out of the month — sometimes more. That's a lot of time! Back then, they didn't pay as much for a speech, and I had to do more of them to make a living . . . I'd have to do about three speeches back then to get the kind of fee you can get for one speech today.

64

I would try to limit the number of speaking engagements I would accept to leave enough time for my family. Birthdays and holidays — Thanksgiving and Christmas — were for family. Trudy and I would mark off time on the calendar for a birthday for one of the kids, or a holiday, and we would set that time aside. Although I hated to turn down engagements because I knew it was money I could use for the family, I'd have to have self-discipline and courage about it.

Being able to duplicate yourself through records, cassettes, videos, books and training courses was also new when I started out. When I was able to sell educational materials, I started making about $10 for every dollar I'd make in speaking fees. Educational materials were relatively new back then, and they turned out to be a terrific source of income for me. Due to the sale of these materials, I could afford to cut my schedule back a little bit.

■   ■   ■

LIFE LESSONS, PASSIONS, BELIEFS AND LEGACY

WHAT IS THE GREATEST LESSON YOU EVER LEARNED?

I think the most significant lesson in my life was the process of finding out what I really wanted to do as a profession. I learned to love speaking, but there was no such thing as a professional speaker back in that day and time. I eventually learned how to make a living at it many years later, but I found that the process of aligning my talents and interests with a form of service to others was the most significant learning process I would ever go through. I learned that you had to ask yourself a series of questions.

- First, you've got to find out if there is a need, an opportunity. In my case, I asked, "Is there a need for training in the real estate field?" or "Is there a need for speakers to learn how to get on the circuit?" So, you need to ask, "What is the need?" and "What is the opportunity?"

- Second: "Am I qualified to do it?"

- Third: "If I'm not qualified to do it, what must I do to get myself qualified?"

- Fourth: "Could I make a living doing it?"

- Fifth: "Would I enjoy it? Would I be challenged by it, and would I be able to stay with it for the rest of my life?"

Find out what field of life you're interested in . . . what field of thought you'd want to enter — something that your life is built around, that you are most interested in. Maybe you'll change your mind later, but try to narrow it down to specifics now. Choose a field that is lasting, not temporary . . . dynamic enough, powerful enough to last. I think that's the most important thing any person can outline.

I went into quite a few different areas in my professional career. After practicing law in New York City, I went to Jerome and Douglas, Arizona, and then to Phoenix, I was with the Industrial Commission for a while, then I was with the Hill brothers practicing law for a while. When I went with the real estate department, I wrote the real estate act, gave all the real estate examinations and got to know all the real estate trainers in the state of Arizona. While I was in the law practice with Dix Price, I had several clients and was attorney for the Phoenix Real Estate Association. I was invited all around the country to talk about real estate and to do sales training.

While involved with real estate, I worked on zoning for cemeteries, and that was how I got into the cemetery business, selling "pre-need" plots. You could buy them at a third of the regular price, so it really made sense. We developed a few cemeteries and put out a weekly paper. One of the first sales training products I ever produced was a combination filmstrip and record set that showed salespeople how to sell pre-need cemetery plots. I started the

Arizona Cemetery Association, which was one of my clients for a while. I went into speaking gradually as I built experience in different fields and began to recognize business problems I was able to help others solve.

WHAT DO YOU STAND FOR?

I like to feel I will leave certain ideas — whether they be in book form, in audiotape or videotape form, or in speeches I've made — that will make this world a little better and help people solve their problems. I really do want to see the whole philosophy of speaking and writing continue, and I like to feel that I contributed a little bit to that. I look back, and I want to make sure I contributed things that are helpful in people's living, not just in making money.

I think it's fine for people to get paid for the work they do, but I like to feel that I have influenced certain people who want to influence other people — kind of a ripple effect . . . on and on and on. If you want to help people, you've "gotta wanna" . . . you've got to have the passion of a lover, the fire of a crusader, the dedication of a saint and the perseverance of a martyr. I'd like to feel I left the world a little better than it was when I entered it.

WHAT WERE YOU HOPING I WOULDN'T ASK YOU?

I was hoping you wouldn't ask me questions that were frustrating rather than questions I could answer and feel like I had the right answer for. There are so many questions — even yet, at my age — that confuse me, such as, "What are some of the things I taught people that I wish I hadn't taught them?" and "What are some of the things I got people to follow that I look at now and think are wrong?" I think one answer to both of those questions is teaching people how they could make more money when what I should have tried to teach them was how they could contribute to the lives of other people, enabling both parties to live happier, healthier lives.

WAS THERE EVER A TIME IN YOUR PROFESSIONAL LIFE WHEN YOU BECAME DISCOURAGED? IF SO, HOW DID YOU OVERCOME YOUR SENSE OF DESPAIR?

One of the times I became very discouraged was when I was with the company in Douglas, Arizona, and the president at the time was very concerned that so many of the little cities wanted to go into the utility business themselves. He encouraged a number of us at Arizona Edison to buy some stock. He thought if we got control of it, he wouldn't lose it. In so many instances, bigger companies were coming in and buying up the small companies and consolidating them.

I started getting my friends to buy the company's stock. It just so happened that the best man at my wedding, a multimillionaire, and another dear friend I had made back in New York had money they had inherited, and they started buying the stock. Shortly thereafter, the president of my company had a board meeting, and he accused me of trying to take over the company. All I was trying to do was to carry out what he had encouraged us to do . . . I didn't realize we would be so successful!

Because of the stock situation, the president wanted to fire me. I became very discouraged, because I felt I had been wrongly accused and misunderstood. Another company came in and saw that this was very valuable stock and offered three or four times as much as my friends had paid for their shares. Rather than spend years in a big proxy fight, I decided to repay my friends by telling them about the offer. They sold their stock to the other company.

That was a discouraging time and a period of adjustment for me. But I got my friends their money back and then some. It was also a sad time for Trudy and me. When we came to Phoenix, we didn't have any money or anyplace to stay and hardly enough to eat. We lived in a little motel on Grand Avenue for a while.

My first two children, JoAnn and Cavett Jr., both became very sick. At the time, we didn't even have a car to take them to the doctor. Dr. Schoffman, a good pediatrician who had been recommended to us, made a call on us. We loved him for that, and he was the pediatrician for all five of our children.

I applied for several jobs around the state. I was appointed as a member of the Industrial Commission, and they gave me what was considered a good salary at the time. Having been a lawyer, I would sit in on hearings of the commission and eventually was made chairman of it.

Most people working in state jobs were appointed by the governor. I remember so well a fellow who worked for one of the candidates for governor, handling his PR. He was such a nice fellow, and he admired me and came to me and said, "I've talked to the boss about you, and if you will quit speaking on behalf of the other candidate, he guarantees you will keep your job at the Industrial Commission if he is elected."

I didn't think it would be right to back out of my support for the other candidate, because I had gotten some friends involved in the campaign. But sure enough, the other candidate was elected. I was told I was going to be let go and that if I wanted to save face, I should resign.

Upon resigning from the Industrial Commission, I joined up with two other lawyers, Roland and George Hill, who had also supported the unsuccessful candidate for governor. We formed a law firm by the name of Hill, Robert and Hill. Later we took in Dix Price.

While in the law firm, I was attorney for many of the auto dealers in the area. They were ready to form an association, and I helped organize the Arizona Automobile Dealers Association and became their first executive director and also their attorney. Many of the dealers would use Hill, Robert, Hill and Price as their attorneys. After about a year working with the auto dealers, I decided I wanted to get back to having a salary. I had a lot of mouths to feed!

I went to the guy who was the head of the land department of the state at the time and tried to show him that they needed to set up a state real estate department. He became very enthused about it but said he thought it would take a long time. I got a bunch of the big firms to give me letters of approval and say how it was necessary and so forth.

During that time, there was a lot of land fraud in Arizona, and we had to have hearings. *Reader's Digest* wrote an article on the land fraud . . . they interviewed me about it and gave me some big publicity. I was invited by the real estate associations to speak all over the United States about land fraud and how the real estate associations should organize and have ethical branches. These associations were my main audience, plus I spoke to the National Real Estate Association many times.

WHAT WAS THE MOST SIGNIFICANT LESSON YOU EVER LEARNED?

Trudy says it was "losing my shirt" on Rancho Grande, the hotel we bought down in southern Arizona. It seemed like a fantastic opportunity at the time. It was a run-down hotel, and I got it very cheap. A good many conventions were held there. It was during World War II, and after I bought the hotel, the government put a cap on what hotels could charge for a room. With the government regulating prices, I could have the hotel filled and not even be able to break even. I lost hundreds of thousands of dollars over two-and-a-half years, and we had to sell it.

We did, however, have some fun while we owned it. I had a plane I used to fly back and forth from Phoenix . . . I'd fly down there at daylight and fly back at night. The hotel had nice rooms, and it was exciting when the movie studios were making movies down there. The studios didn't have to pay union scale down there like they did in California.

We had stables at Rancho Grande that were used to keep horses for the movies. John Wayne was making *Red River* at the time, and he stayed there. I got to be a good friend of his. In fact, I used to invite a lot of my friends to stay there . . . I wasn't making any money, but I figured I may as well have some fun!

Finally, I bumped into John Mills, who owned the Westward Ho in Phoenix and told him my situation with the Rancho Grande. He said, "It looks like you're not going to make a dime, or even be able to break even, as long as this price-control law is in effect." I said, "What would you give me for the thing?" He said, "The only way I could make it work would be to subdivide some of it into cottages and homes." He put up $10,000 cash and I had some bills to pay off, so I ended up with practically nothing.

It was discouraging, but I was much younger then and had a great spirit of adventure. Everything was a challenge to me. The involvement with the movies was exciting, and I'd enjoy flying my plane down there two or three times a week.

When the actress Ann Lee came to Phoenix to open the Sombrero Playhouse, she needed help, and someone suggested she see me. I got real excited about it and got several people to put up money for her. I was on the playhouse board, and Ann would see to it that I met all the movie people when they came to town.

When Ann got the president of the bank and title company interested in the playhouse, they raised about $25,000. They had some connection with the prison and were able to use the help of the prisoners to build the Sombrero Playhouse.

The playhouse was seeking people to be in its plays, and Ann asked me to be in a couple of them. I would get the gist of what I was supposed to say and then kind of improvise. The other actors found this difficult, because they couldn't get their cues from me. I remember Ann came up to me after such an instance and said, "Cavett, I've never seen anything like it in my life . . . you rewrote that whole scene!" I responded, "Well, Ann, you didn't tell me I had to say it exactly like it was written!" I was just informal about it, and when I thought of something else to say, I'd say it. Cavett Jr. took a big part in one of the plays.

Through Ann, I met JoAnn Drew and John Ireland, who decided they wanted to open a tennis resort down there. Jim Herron, who had owned a utility company in Miami, Arizona, decided he wanted to take the thing over and make me general manager. We called it The Racquet Club.

I worked very hard at The Racquet Club and got to know a lot of the people. Eventually, I formed the Tennis Patrons Association and the International Junior Tennis Association. We ultimately attracted 1,500 members to The Racquet Club, each of whom paid $15 a month in membership fees. Cavett Jr. was a very good tennis player, and so was my younger son, Wicky. We had a lot of fun with it. Eventually, some movie people bought it and now it's called John Gardner's Tennis Ranch.

WHY DO YOU THINK CONTRIBUTING TO OTHERS' LIVES IS SO IMPORTANT?

I know a lot of people . . . I'm not criticizing them, but they promote their sales presentations by saying, "I guarantee I can teach you to make more money!" and people sign up thinking, "They're going to teach me to be successful." I prefer a pitch with the tone, "If you come in, I will give you a method for developing yourself to the point where you can help people with their problems. As a by-product, you'll have an income that's secure."

I think it's so important to know that the ability to influence people can be a dangerous thing as well as a blessing. Some speakers want to influence others to pursue a "get rich quick" scheme rather than to help other people substantially. I think these speakers can be dangerous, because they try to sell people on the idea, "Come and pay me so much money, and I'm going to teach you to be successful," and they have the wrong idea of what success is. They figure they are going to teach people how to make a lot more money, when really what you want to teach is how to influence people for betterment.

You said earlier that one of the things that gives you joy and passion in living is being able to have a secure income . . .

. . . derived from *helping* people, an income from the right thing. You then get the sincere feeling, "I am helping other people." There isn't any feeling that is greater, more substantial, longer lasting or more fulfilling in life than knowing you solved people's problems in the right way. It doesn't just bring happiness, it brings a kind of blessedness.

What, specifically, has given you joy and passion in living?

Next to helping other people, the spiritual things of life and my family, I think one of the things is a realization of my financial ambitions. I don't want to sound selfish, like I've tried to see how much I can get. But I want to be financially secure and keep my present standard of living, and I can say truthfully that I want it as much for my loved ones, for my wife, as I want it for myself. I want to be financially secure and to know, when I get to the point where I can't make any more money — I've just about reached the stage where I don't have speaking engagements that I am paid for — that I am accumulating enough that is self-sustaining, where the interest on the money and various things will see that I have this security.

Certainly, speaking in front of an audience and helping people solve their problems have given me great joy and passion over the years. I feel like it's a dual thing: Not only am I getting paid and accumulating some money, but I figure I am helping solve people's problems while I'm doing it. I think it's a realization of what Dr. Peale said: "The only rent we pay for the space we occupy while we're on this earth is helping other people solve their problems." He elaborated, saying if there is a spark of divinity, a fragment of eternity, a gamble with immortality on this earth, it is found in helping others solve their problems. And in so doing, you solve one of your own problems: You accumulate enough money that you can relax and enjoy life, watching others accomplish their ambitions.

Do the same things give you joy and passion now?

I worked a long time and passed up Social Security benefits until I got into the secondary phase of retirement. By that time, I had accumulated a little stock that pays dividends, and it gives me the greatest pleasure to see that I am getting enough to live on without having to do a lot of work, as I used to do. It isn't that I want to get away from my work . . . it's the fact that life is passing on, where these things now are the responsibilities and enjoyment of people much younger than I. Moving into an area of living that is enjoyable and that is a realization of my financial ambitions gives me pleasure.

When I was younger, I lived such a wild, fitful, feverish existence. Now, simple things give me so much pleasure. When you get to be a certain age, a great door of happiness and enjoyment opens up to you that was closed when you were younger. In fact, it's so great, you almost feel sorry for younger people! Music sounds better, you enjoy friends more, you have a sensitivity— food even tastes better . . . believe you me, it does!

One thing, too . . . you enjoy imaginative things more than you ever did. Not that you're living in a fantasy world, but you can imagine certain things and appreciate them. You're more sensitive to certain things and have a sense of fulfillment and satisfaction in your mind that you never had as a younger person. When you are younger, you want more and more and more—"How will I accomplish this or that?"

You get to a point . . . not where you retire and you don't want to have certain things, or you want to die young — you know that great ol' expression, "Please don't let me die until I'm dead" . . . but to a point where you enjoy what you have coming and feel like it is a fulfillment. You don't need as much to feel fulfilled as you did when you were younger. I think the Lord gives you a gift of enjoyment that you don't have earlier in life.

Now, getting older hasn't swayed me from my belief that exaggeration makes life more interesting. It isn't that you want to lie about things, but you can kind of romanticize things by telling stories. Trudy always says that I love being the oldest person in a group because I can tell a story and there are no eye witnesses to ruin it! These days, I even enjoy listening to others' stories as much as I used to enjoy telling them myself.

We have a prayer group that meets on Wednesday mornings . . . there are 12 of us . . . and I decided to start wearing my hearing aids to the meetings because I was missing so much of what was being said, and I wanted to participate. When I wore the hearing aids, however, I realized that I became even more quiet, because the things I was hearing were so much more important and meaningful than anything I wanted to say. I've become a listener instead of a talker . . . that's quite a graduation for a speaker!

The older I get, the more I enjoy sitting in an audience and hearing someone else speak. It can be truths I've heard a dozen times, but I enjoy hearing them, and I believe in them and know they are true. It used to be that I would question certain ideas, certain beautiful thoughts. I would think, "Is that true? I hope it is." Now I know these things are true, and when you are certain that things are true, you enjoy them a lot more than when you are wondering if they are true or not. It's another "graduation."

WHAT DO YOU BELIEVE HAPPENS WHEN YOU DIE?

I went to my weekly prayer group yesterday at the church, and we talked about that. Suddenly everyone turned around to me . . . I think it was because they thought I'd be faced with death before they were! I told them this is something that, the more you think about it, the more questions you have.

I used to worry about the afterlife when I was a youngster down in Mississippi. I remember the pastor, a foot-washing Baptist, would say, "If you come up and shake hands, join the church and give your life to Christ, you will live in eternal bliss. If you don't, you will burn in hell for all eternity!" He said that if a little child dies before joining the church, he'll burn in hell. My mother would say that she didn't believe that was true, but it used to frighten me so! Religion was more or less something I was afraid of.

The more afraid I was, the more I would study the Bible, and I found out this: The more you study the Bible, the more unanswered questions you have. I think that's where the old expression "Truth is a whole and fragmentation, an error" comes in. You've got to look at the whole pattern of life and death to understand it, rather than pick out some little phase.

You are always going to find things you can't understand, and that's where faith comes in. The more questions you have about eternity, the more unanswered questions you'll have. That's when you need faith and turn to faith. The Bible says, "Faith is the substance of things hoped for, the evidence of things not seen."

Someone at our prayer group brought up the question, "Will people who don't believe in God go to heaven or have eternal life?" And I liked the way someone else answered. She said, "You know, God is going to take care of everyone. We don't go to heaven because we believe in God, we have eternal life because he believes in us."

One of the things that impressed me so much was that my brother Pierre, who died the other day at 94, wrote a letter . . . he knew he was going to pass away . . . saying, "I hope you won't be jealous of me that I get to be in heaven with our friends and loved ones long before you, but I'll tell them that you'll be coming along one of these days and to save a place for you."

It reminded me of something Dr. Peale said about resurrection and passing away — that all of existence is a matter of birth and so-called death. You are born from your mother's womb and when you are born, it is a death from the womb and you start living an earthly existence. Then, you die out of childhood and are born into middle age. Eventually, you die out of middle age and are born into older age. And finally, the greatest blessing of all is when you pass from this earth and are born into permanent existence, joining all of your loved ones who died before you. Your funeral should not be about people getting together to share the sorrow of losing someone but getting together to remember all the great times they had with you and the fact that you are born into eternal spiritual happiness and that they will be rejoined with you someday.

Whatever is ahead, it couldn't be more of a miracle than that we are here in the first place. My wife's mother was a very religious person, full of faith, and was always looked upon as a leader in the church. When people would ask her, "What do you think will happen when we pass from this earth?" she would always say, "I know things are going to be great, but I'm not on the committee for arrangements!"

71

DID YOU HAVE ANY BELIEFS YOU GREW UP WITH THAT, AS YOU BECAME A MAN, YOU CHANGED YOUR MIND ABOUT?

When I was growing up, hunting was such a great sport. I used to go hunting with my brother Pierre and with Charlie Tabb, who raised hounds . . . he had great bird dogs. I used to go hunting more to be with the people than to shoot the animals. I eventually got to the point where I couldn't shoot a deer anymore. I remember a deer wandered into our camp when everyone but me was asleep, and I shooed it away because I was afraid someone was going to wake up and shoot it. That deer was so beautiful . . . I couldn't hunt them anymore after that.

Another thing that came to affect me strongly was how black people were treated in the South. When I was growing up, there was not as much awareness of the differences between Northerners and Southerners as there was about the differences between black people and white people. But generations of black people would live with white families as cooks, servants and the like, and we were all very close.

As I got older, I didn't want to criticize my parents, but I could never understand their feelings toward black people . . . they always seemed to feel the differences between the races. But I felt so close to Charlie Tabb and loved him and his wife, Annie, so much that skin color just didn't seem to matter. There were very few people I admired as much as Charlie Tabb. He took me hunting, and Mother called him my "hunting father."

I remember one time I lost my knife, and I said to Charlie, "Charlie, did I loan you my knife?" and he said, "Yes, you did," and he gave it back to me. I was so relieved, I went to Mother and cried, saying, "I thought Charlie had stolen my knife," a thought that nearly broke my heart, because I trusted him so. I was so very sensitive. I was the youngest in the family, and malaria fever kept me out of school a lot, so I guess that made me a little more sensitive.

DID YOUR CONCEPT OF MASCULINITY CHANGE OVER THE COURSE OF YOUR LIFE? IF SO, HOW?

I don't believe any kid can be reared on a college campus and not have an insane admiration for athletes. I remember Billie Hayes coached the Gatchell kid, the Javelin thrower who entered the Olympics. He also coached a runner named Murphy and another runner — one ran the 220 and the 100, and one ran the mile. I admired them so, and I admired the baseball players . . . I remember Coach Chadwick. I admired them all.

Even when I got into college, I admired the athletes. But when I got out into the business world, I realized there were other things much more important than being an athlete. When I worked for a big law firm in New York City — which eventually became Beekman, Bogue, Leek, Stevens and Black — there were seven of us in this big room, and we each had a desk. It was then that I got so I admired people who were successful in their profession.

Back in that day and time, we had our senior partners, and I knew what they were all earning. The junior partners would do a lot of the work, but the older people who attracted and brought in the clients were the ones making the big money. The junior partners would do the trial work, and the senior partners would sit back and bring in the clients — people their age they'd been friends with all their lives.

Then I got to the point where I admired people in the banks and big companies who were selling stock. A whole new revelation came to me when I entered the business world. Prior to that time, I had lived on a college campus, as either a professor's son or a student, all my life.

When we talk about change, we must realize there are two phases of change. One is a change in the system and the culture's way of doing things — this is true in all facets of life and industry. The other change is in ourselves, in harmonizing with these changes in the system or culture. Very few people are aware of these two phases of change, but we can't solve problems relating to change unless we consider both phases important and deal with change both externally and internally.

In response to your question, the whole basis of judging masculinity and femininity has changed so much over the years. When I was growing up, you hardly ever heard of women in business —in teaching, but that's about all. Even before you started school, women were your primary teachers — the mother and maybe the grandmother. Then, until you were in the eighth or ninth grade, all the teachers were women. A woman had to rear the children, learn to cook and learn to sew . . . that was her role, completely.

When you pick up the paper today, you read about women running for office, women in business, women taking college courses to prepare themselves for business . . . even women in the military. Sixty percent of the people starting small businesses today are women.

It's now getting to where women's and men's roles are changing completely, according to the needs of society. You hear very little about "masculinity" these days, whereas there used to be such a contrast between men and women. Nowadays, the duties, obligations and opportunities for women and men are nearly the same.

I'll never forget the first time I tried a lawsuit before a female judge in New York City. These days, of course, many judges are women, but it was rare back then. I got up there and was at first concerned with being polite, feeling obligated to be gentlemanly in front of her. Then she called me down a couple of times and directed me, and I realized that I had to be on a 50-50 basis with her. It was a big shock to me! I'll also never forget the first time I went to a Dale Carnegie course taught by a woman. It took me a little time to give her the respect I should and to realize that she was speaking authoritatively.

So, right now, we are dealing with all kinds of societal, or external, changes. But even though we've all accepted the fact of tremendous change in society, we are almost completely ignoring the important secondary phase of change — changing ourselves to adjust to the outer changes!

I'll never forget the first time I saw a woman mail carrier. It used to be only men would deliver the mail. I was challenged . . . I knew I had to adjust myself, and there was a period of adjustment. People today don't have this problem as much, because women mail carriers aren't the novelty today that they were back then.

For a long time, women didn't assert themselves. They accepted the fact that their duty, their place in society, was to rear the children, make a beautiful home, encourage their husband and so forth. Now women have just as much ambition to assume important positions in business, politics and society as men do.

When a man and woman marry today, often the woman has an income and is professionally ambitious. Men today find that with inflation and prices so high, it is very convenient to have a two-income family. Rather than having the woman spend all of her time looking after the home, like it used to be, a family is able to hire people to help look after the home. Until recently, few people had maids that came in. One of the major factors in the growth of cleaning services was the inception of the two-income family.

I haven't had this feeling of change so much between Trudy and me, because whenever you have a great love and affection, you don't become as analytical about it as you do with other people. When I met Trudy, she was an academician . . . I met her when she was in college. We've always respected each other's views, even if they have not always been the same. In the last few years, Trudy says I've wanted our views to be the same and that I want her to be the one to determine them . . . particularly financially.

WITHIN YOUR OWN MARRIAGE, WHAT FACTORS PROMOTED THE SHARING OF FINANCIAL DECISIONS?

One thing was that I went into a phase of work where I was away from home so much that someone besides me needed to make these decisions. Furthermore, Trudy was very qualified, because she had gone to college and had handled her own finances. Before I went into business for myself, I had my secretary pay our family's bills. Trudy was glad to take that over, because she liked knowing where the money was going.

Interest rates were high back then, and we made quite a little money on certificates of deposit . . . so I felt Trudy was really smart! She was always very organized, and we eventually came to realize that she handled our finances much better than I ever did!

WHAT IS THE SOURCE OF YOUR BEAUTIFUL, LOVING PHILOSOPHY?

One of the blessings I grew up with is that I always had a very inquiring mind. I had an inferiority complex growing up, having been born into a family where there had been a lot of academic success— my father was a college dean and professor, and one of my brothers was a college president. Plus, my wife's father was a college professor. I had a very inquiring mind and knew that I would have to learn a lot to get into the league they were in. I realized that to be a success, I had a long ways to go . . . and I developed an inquiring mind.

WHY DO YOU LOVE PEOPLE SO MUCH AND SO CONSISTENTLY?

Trudy jokes about this, quoting me as saying, "I love mankind . . . it's *people* I can't stand!" But I do enjoy people, and although I wasn't brilliant in an academic way, I found out that the thing that really counts in life is the "people business."

■　　　■　　　■

I came from a whole family of teachers — people who worked with people . . . who were in the people business. I found that I got a great sense of satisfaction offering services to people. When people need my help, it's more than an incentive for me to listen to them and encourage them. I get a great deal of satisfaction out of helping people.

Sometimes I bite off more than I can chew. If I get to the point where I realize I cannot help a person, then I think the best thing I can do is fade out of their situation without hurting their feelings or criticizing them or running them down. In some instances, I've wanted to help people . . . and thought I was helping them . . . and then later found out they were beyond my help. Then the thing to do is try to fade out of their lives without hurting their feelings or discouraging them. It's not an easy thing to do.

You should be very careful, if you are going to devote yourself to being a mentor, that you know as much about a person's background as you can so you don't get into the middle of things and then have to walk out. You want to find out: a) if you can help them and b) whether they are likely to respond to your help. If you do that and find you cannot help them, you must try to get out in a way that avoids hurting them. I've had someone say, "Well, you were going to help me. If you aren't going to help me, I'm through!" You've got to fade out in a way that helps reinstate their belief in themselves and encourages them to get another mentor. As I say, it's not an easy thing to do.

WHAT WAS THE MOST INSPIRATIONAL MOMENT OF YOUR LIFE?

I was asked to speak at a joint meeting of the house of representatives and the senate in my home state of Mississippi years and years ago. When I got through, I read a little poem that I had written, *The Creed of the Great American*, and dedicated it to them.

74

THE CREED OF THE GREAT AMERICAN

I am proud of my country.

And I believe in the free enterprise system

which made her great.

I'm thankful for my sacred heritage.

And I pledge to do all in my power to protect it.

To this end, I don't want just security, I want opportunity.

I don't want to be a kept citizen.

I don't want others to do for me what I can do for myself.

I seek no career in poverty.

I want to earn my paycheck, not just collect it.

I want to be able to hope and dream and take chances.

Yes, and even fail, and with the nobility of a second start, rise and fight to win.

I know that without this challenge, my soul and spirit and all that is within me will shrivel and die.

■   ■   ■

I'll not sell my birthright for a handout.

I'll not exchange my liberty for a dole.

And this I know above all else:

If I cling to these principles, if I hold to these ideas,

    then and only then can I stand erect, with head high,

marching forward to the music of a greater destiny,

facing my flag with good conscience and proudly say,

    "I am an American!"

I believe in my country and her destiny.

I still believe in the original dreams

    of our founding fathers.

I shall keep faith with my sacred heritage.

I was very sentimental about speaking at this event because I had a lot of relatives in Mississippi. The governor had declared it "Cavett Robert Day" throughout the state, and they gave me a certificate and put my speech and poem in the records of the joint meeting of the Mississippi house of representatives and senate.

In my speech, I said that no nation has ever turned communist, socialist or fascist until it's done three things: gotten control of the country's means of communication, taken control of the country's educational system to shape the thinking of its youth and destroyed the great desire within people to participate in and help build their country. I went on to say that one of the things I fight against more than anything else is this thinking I call "let George do it."

'Let George Do It'

I think the greatest thing that any of us can do is to get a little more involved in community affairs. You can't outgive a community. I don't mean do these things for any naked, selfish interest or any anticipation you may get from the community of favors yet to come. But please don't be like I am. I'm getting to the point where when anyone says, "Will you do something . . . serve on a committee, join this or that?" . . . I say, "Look, I have more than I can say grace over now . . . let George do it." You see, there's always some knucklehead by the name of George around, and he'll represent us.

I like the story of the little fellow who was 5'2" who went up to the fellow who was 6'6" and said, "You know, if I was as big as you are, you know what I'd do? I'd go out in the woods, I'd find myself the biggest bear I could, and I'd tear him to pieces." The big fellow looked at the little fellow and said, "Son, there are a lot of little bears out in them there woods, too."

So many of us think that if we can't head up a department, why should we get involved? "If I can't be on the city commission, why should I build for good citizenship?" "If I can't head

■   ■   ■

the chamber of commerce, why should I get out and try to build my city?"

Remember the little old fellow in his 90s who said, "I'm only one, but I am one. I cannot do everything, but I can do something. And I'll not let what I cannot do interfere with what I can do. So while I can run, I'll run; while I can walk, I'll walk; when I can only crawl, I'll crawl. But by the grace of God, I'll always be moving forward."

I want to just point out two or three historical figures and what they would've sounded like trying to pawn off their memorable acts on hapless Georges.

You take this guy called Nathan Hale. Now, what did ol' Nate mean when he said, "I regret that I have but one life to give for my country"? You know what Nate could have said? "Me, spy on the British? Are you trying to be funny? You know what they do with spies? They hang 'em! Let George get his neck stretched . . . that's not my cup of tea."

Ol' Paul Revere could so easily have said, "Ride through every Middlesex village in the county, and in the middle of the night? Am I the only guy in Boston who's got a horse? No! Let George do it!"

Even Patrick Henry should have had his head examined when he said, "Give me liberty or give me death." You know what Pat could have said? "Sure, pal . . . I'm for liberty: first, last and always. But we've got to be realistic, friend . . . we're a pretty small outfit. We go pushing the British around, somebody's gonna get hurt, and it ain't gonna be me. I'll tell you what I did . . . I just wrote a beautiful little speech on liberty. Let George read it to the Assembly."

One of the greatest privileges I ever had was speaking at a banquet in Houston honoring the Apollo X crew of astronauts. I have never met such a great group of people in my life. I've gotten to know some of them rather intimately, including Tom Stafford and John Young. They are too precious to send to the moon. If we could take these great people, these great Americans, put them on our school campuses for one day and let our young people see what great Americans are like — talk with them, rub elbows with them, mix with them — I think we'd change the climate overnight.

Every one of those brave individuals wants to go to the moon. You know what I would have said? "Hey, diddle-diddle! Didn't you see what happened to Apollo 13? Didn't you see what happened to the Space Shuttle? Let George do it!"

I'm always so proud when I face a bunch of Georges. I would like to ask you what you think George would say about our country. I think he might send us home with a question like this . . .

What is America, anyway? And just who is Uncle Sam? Do we ever think of who Uncle Sam is? He isn't the Army, he isn't the Navy, he isn't the tax collector, he isn't the homeless person on the corner, he isn't the mob coming down the street. But he's a lot of people, both living and dead, and something that lives within us.

■   ■   ■

Uncle Sam's a fellow who thumbed his nose at the Redcoats and dumped a whole boatload of tea in the Boston Harbor. He's the bandy-legged youth, Benjamin Franklin, who walked into Philadelphia with a pack of dogs at his heels and remained to establish a reputation as America's most eminent statesman and scientist. Uncle Sam's a little band of patriots at Valley Forge, shivering in the winter snow, with all hope of victory gone . . . holding on to life itself to give us the sacred heritage we enjoy today.

He's the homely, unhappy boy in the woods of Illinois who failed and failed so many times yet, through sheer faith, emerged so great a man he wrote the Gettysburg Address. He's Susan B. Anthony, Charles Kettering, Eleanor Roosevelt, Madam Curie, Henry Ford, Thomas Edison, the spirit of Walter Chrysler . . . people with strong spirits and tough brains who made free enterprise a word that frightened little dictators.

Uncle Sam is simply the best of you and me and what we want this country to be: free, brave and strong. He's you and me and millions of other Americans who are willing to sacrifice, willing to work hard to keep this country the greatest thing on the face of this earth.

I had always worshiped my grandfather, "Pappy," who was involved with the Mississippi legislature. For me, being invited to speak to the joint meeting of the house and senate of the Mississippi legislature and having them declare "Cavett Robert Day" in the state of Mississippi was like going to heaven. It made me feel like I'd "arrived."

IF YOU COULD RECOMMEND ONLY THREE BOOKS, WHAT WOULD THEY BE?

My favorites were *The Three Musketeers*, as a child, and, as an adult, Dr. Peale's *The Power of Positive Thinking* and Napoleon Hill's *Think and Grow Rich*.

HOW DID YOU KEEP YOUR ZEST FOR LIFE FOR 87 YEARS?

Fortunately, I worshiped so many people. I was the youngest in the family, and I had older brothers who were so talented and successful, and Dr. Gaines was such a great speaker. More than anything else, I wanted to follow in the footsteps of these people I admired so much. I never followed dry, academic principles; I wanted to be like certain people. I don't think there is anyone I know who has patterned his life so much after certain people he loved and admired as I have — not only in my youth, but all throughout my life . . . even now.

The older you get, the more you love and appreciate people and the more you want to grasp their example and the principles they live by. I never grasp principles independent of a person — they're always connected. That was the thing that made me believe so strongly in the concept of mentors and mentees — it worked with me, and I figured if I passed that along to other people, it would have the same impact. That's why I've always felt that if you can influence people, that's the greatest thing you can do.

WHAT HELPED YOU KEEP THE VISION OF ALL THAT YOU DESIRED?

If ever you can fall in love with what you are doing, it will propel you like nothing else. They say ambition is one thing but if you've got a vision in life, it's the most powerful thing in the world. You never get rid of that . . . it attracts you in a way that no ambition or plans can ever do. A vision is so powerful — it's everything about you that is craving certain things. Ambition is ideas you hope you can learn and repeat to other people. But vision is permanent and will create in you things that ambition never could.

I had ambitions about speaking that finally became visions. I wanted to be like my brother-in-law and my older brothers, and I longed for that for so long that at some point, it just seemed to grasp me and take hold of me. That feeling was so powerful, it will continue to attract me for as long as I live.

Every time I found some idea or some message that would help me in realizing my vision as a speaker, it would grab me. When you get a vision, you don't have to seek ideas . . . ideas seek you. When you run across something you're reading and it falls in line with your vision, it becomes a part of you . . . you write it down and fit it in with your message. I think a lot of people don't realize the difference between ambition and a vision in life. Ambition is when you are seeking certain things, but vision becomes a part of you . . . it's almost like a second person inside of you giving you advice — a higher power.

YOU ARE SUCH A SHARP DRESSER. WHERE DID YOU LEARN THIS FINE ART, AND WHO, IF ANYONE, INFLUENCED YOUR SENSE OF STYLE?

Where I come from in Mississippi, you didn't have to try to win a beauty contest every time you went out of the house. I wore overalls to grammar school . . . that was fancy dressing down there. Then when I went to high school, I wore jeans. There were three boys in my family, and we couldn't afford fancy clothes. You'd never have more than one suit of clothes.

When I went away to college, it was different. Everybody dressed well, and you wanted to be one of them. I remember it was 10 cents to have a suit pressed. Sometimes I didn't have enough money, so I'd iron it myself and shine my own shoes. As you got into business, people would kind of judge you by the clothes you wore, and you always had to be well-shaven and have a good haircut.

When I finally got into the speaking business, I had to dress immaculately. That's when Trudy started helping me choose my clothes. I used to go and hear people speak, and I came to realize that you were the message yourself. You had to use effective gestures and be well-dressed . . . it was a physical, mental and emotional performance. If you were not dressed well and you talked about excellence in a field, people would not believe what you had to say.

I was smart enough to know that Trudy was a real expert in the field of tasteful dress — colors harmonizing together and so on — and I relied heavily on her counsel in these matters. I started asking her which tie I should wear with which suit. In the professional field, they would put on seminars to tell you how to look professional and dress well.

HOW DO YOU DEAL WITH YOUR BODY WHEN IT STOPS FUNCTIONING AS WELL AS IT USED TO?

You grow strong in the "crucible of adversity." There are very few people who ever attain greatness except through trials and tribulations and adjusting to disappointments. There are two big adjustments you have to make when your body stops functioning well: You've got to adjust your environment and physical activities, and you've got to adjust yourself — your emotional state.

When I lived in the South, I had malaria fever when I was a teenager. I don't think I ever would have gotten over it if I hadn't left Mississippi and gone up to South Carolina. I was terribly disappointed that I couldn't do my athletics, and I had to look to other things. If you run into something you can't deal with, you've got to substitute something else for it . . . otherwise, you'll just die on the vine.

When I went to New York to practice law, I started having so many sinus and lung problems that the doctors gave me six months and sent me to Arizona to die. I was so disappointed, because I had been working with Tom Dewey and the racket investigations and felt I was really moving up in the world.

When I got to the West, I had an operation on my sinuses. Afterwards, they became infected, and I almost didn't make it. Trudy said that when I was delirious, I said, "I want to see my momma before I die . . . I want to see my momma before I die." I did get well, however, and start to thrive in the dry climate. I took up golf and won the state amateur golf tournament.

So, you've got to make two big adjustments whenever your body malfunctions: You've got to have a change in your environment and also an adjustment in your attitude. If I had moved to Arizona but not tried to take care of myself, I wouldn't have gotten better. Or if I'd stayed in New York and taken good care of myself, it wouldn't have mattered, either. It took a combination of changing my environment and making an adjustment in my attitude.

More recently in my life, I had a heart attack. In the first place, I had to quit living such an active life, whereas I used to travel all over the world. There were times when I used to get home one day, then leave the same day for somewhere else. I had to learn to harmonize my activities within the parameters of my physical condition.

I got to the point where I was very dissatisfied with my body. I would try to take good care of it and get more sleep, but it wouldn't react the way I thought it should. So, I knew it was a permanent condition . . . they call it AGE.

WHAT HELPS KEEP YOUR ATTITUDE OPTIMISTIC ABOUT THE 'GOLDEN YEARS'?

I've been thinking, What has changed in this phase of my life to make it so enjoyable? I feel that now I have time to "stop and smell the flowers along the way" a little bit more. I was sitting here looking out the window today, and I have come to a great acceptance of the feeling that you don't have to own something to enjoy it.

Looking out the window at the beautiful campus lawn here at the Beatitudes, I realize that I would had to have had hundreds of millions of dollars to own something like I am looking out upon right now. There are 10 or 15 people working out there — mowing the grass and climbing the trees to trim the limbs. I could never have afforded to pay for something like that. And I enjoy it more because I don't have to pay for the upkeep!

A lot of people are so busy accumulating and accumulating that they don't have time to enjoy the things they have. These days, I'm thankful to be able to turn on the TV and find out what's going on in the world without having to pay advisors hundreds of millions of dollars to tell me the day's events in Europe and all around!

We can go to a park or see a sunset or go to a zoo and get enjoyment out of these wonderful things, and we don't have to pay a cent for them. People take many of these things for granted and accept them as just routine. Whenever you figure you don't have to own something to enjoy it, if you can grasp that philosophy, it's a great, great thing.

This morning, when I watched my daughter Lee speak to a group, I enjoyed it 10 times more than if I'd spoken to the group and gotten a standing ovation. You can enjoy things that you don't participate in personally. So, I think these are two important concepts to grasp in life: You don't have to own something to enjoy it, and you can take as much pride in the successes of your loved ones as you do in your own.

HOW DO YOU FEEL ABOUT RETIREMENT?

In 1992, Trudy and I sold our home and moved to the Beatitudes, a retirement community, which we love. Overall, retirement has been a difficult adjustment for me, but with the love of my family and a sense of humor, I've been working on it. My own father died six months after he retired . . . he just didn't know what to do with himself.

When the doctor said I couldn't travel anymore, I was afraid the same thing would happen to me.

But my doctor said that I could "putter around" . . . so I bought a golf club — a putter! — the other day at a yard sale, and I've been using it as a walking cane. It works real well. So, I'm learning to putter around! To me, the putter symbolizes the process of moving from youth to middle age, and the older I get, the more I realize you go back to youth again!

Organizations I have enjoyed as a member during my career and after retirement include NSA, Toastmasters, Lions, Kiwanis, Speakers Roundtable and the Sigma Chi Fraternity. Great friendships!

*Cavett with his father,
Joseph Clark Robert, in 1913*

*Cavett in the front of his house with
his dog, "Sport," and his brother*

Cavett in grade school, 1917

Cavett as a college student in 1927

Cavett with his father, Joseph Clark Robert (right), and his brother Joe (center)

*Cavett with his siblings —
from left, Cavett, Dr. Pierre,
Sadie Duvergne and Dr. Joe*

Cavett and Trudy, married one year, in 1934

Trudy and Cavett, married 50 years, in 1983

Cavett and Trudy: the young newlyweds in New York, 1933

SAN FRANCISCO AREA
AMERICAN SALESMASTERS CONGRESS

$1000.

REV. BOB E. RICHARDS

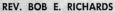

- 2-time Olympic Pole Vault Champion and 3-time U. S. Decathalon winner.
- One of J. C.s "Top Ten Young Men".
- Noted Television and Sports Personality.

Rev. Bob Richards, Olympic pole vault record setter and 3 times U. S. Decathalon champ, has turned his leadership to the field of human relations. Bob has motivated millions with his speeches and book "Heart of a Champion."

$500.

DR. KENNETH McFARLAND

- Honored by U. S. Chamber of Commerce as America's No. 1 Speaker.
- Lecturer and author of ELOQUENCE IN PUBLIC SPEAKING.

Take a man. Gift him with talent, elegant dignity - - - and humility. This will give you some kind of an idea what Dr. Kenneth McFarland, who blends the humor of Will Rogers with the urgency of Churchill, is like.

Dr. McFarland's tremendous speaking demand has brought him the title "America's Top Airline Passenger". His many personal talks, books and records have given inspiration to millions of Americans.

★ ★

$1000.

DR. MAXWELL MALTZ

Few men can be called a legend within their own time. Dr. Maxwell Maltz, internationally renowned author of the book "Psycho-Cybernetics" is one of those few.

Through the media of his book and through his personal appearances Dr. Maltz has influenced the lives of millions of Americans.

$500.

FRED HERMAN

Fred has worked hundreds of times with sales groups all over the U.S.A., Canada, Europe and the Orient. His experience includes selling in many types of business and industry. His Sales Training programs have been featured in motion pictures and on radio and television. Mr. Herman is best known for his ability to provide practical, forceful answers to everyday sales problems. You'll be glad you met him.

★ ★

$350.

CAVETT ROBERT

For over 20 years Mr. Robert has held sales schools and conducted courses in Human Engineering and Personal Development for many of the Nation's outstanding companies. Reader's Digest recently contained an article recognizing his activities.

Mr. Robert's wisdom in sales and Human Relations is drawn from a wide background of experience. He has sold insurance, taught law, insurance, and real estate. He is International Winner of Toastmaster International. He is the author of a Prentice-Hall book and over two dozen inspirational sales recordings.

May 16 and 17, 1968
California Masonic Memorial Temple
1111 California
San Francisco, California

TUITION: $35.00

American Salesmasters, Inc. — JACK TAR SQUARE
1255 POST STREET, SUITE 308
SAN FRANCISCO, CALIFORNIA 94109
PHONE: 885-0515

HOME OFFICE: American Salesmasters • 5827 Outlook • Shawnee Mission, Kansas 66202 • Area Code 913 HE 2-2747

TICKETS BY RESERVATION ON A FIRST-TO-ORDER BASIS...

American Salesmasters Congress brochure, featured speakers and their fees, 1968

Cavett's first publicity photo as a professional speaker (age 60 years)

In 1978, NSA created an award inspired by the work of Cavett Robert — Robert Henry presented its namesake with the first Cavett Award

Merlyn Cundiff and Cavett rehearse a presentation

Cavett receives "The Old Shoe" award, presented by D. John Hammond and given on behalf of 63 top American speakers who wrote letters attesting to the recipients boundless generosity

Cavett being honored by the State of Mississippi with Cavett Robert Day

Cavett, age 53, in Mexico with his mother, Hal, her two sister and his wife, Trudy

Cavett and Trudy with their children

Cavett and Alan Cimberg shared a platform in Florida, 1968

Cavett, age 73, at the height of his career, speaking at Dr. Robert Schuller's Crystal Cathedral

*Cavett gets roasted by Merlyn Cundiff,
in Scottsdale, Arizona,1975*

*The Sixth Annual Phoenix Summer Sales Seminar in
1977 preceded NSA's annual convention where
Cavett received a big "thank you" from Merlyn
Cundiff and Mark Victor Hansen*

*Cavett receives the Golden Gavel Award from
Toastmasters International*

Cavett in his early 70s

Cavett and Lee E. Robert, his daughter and business partner

Cavett with D. John Hammond, his best friend

Cavett in his early 80s

Cavett striking his classic speaking pose

Cavett

THREE SPEECHES

Many people have inquired where they can obtain Dad's books, *The Cavett Robert Personal Development Course* and *Success With People Through Human Engineering and Motivation*. These books are currently out of print, although I hope to republish them in the near future.

The following chapters are borrowed from the *Human Engineering* book and are of particular interest because their content was used for Dad's three most famous speeches. I hope you enjoy them. (Each of these speeches appears in its entirety, exactly as it was originally published.)

SOMETHING
WILL ROGERS SAID

Back in 1935 I had a privilege I shall always cherish.

I was invited to a luncheon as a guest. To my amazement and delight Will Rogers was the speaker. This was one of the last speeches Will Rogers ever made because a few weeks later he and Wiley Post started their flight around the world. We all know the tragic death they met in Alaska.

Now Mr. Rogers did not have the scholarly flavor or the academic taste that one might expect from some of the economic prognosticators of his day. But in a few words he gave some of the most profound advice I have ever heard.

I've read many books on success. I've heard dozens upon dozens of records on this same subject. But I don't believe there is a surer formula or a more certain blueprint leading to success, if followed conscientiously, than this one.

"If you want to be successful," he said, "it's just this simple.

"Know what you are doing.

"Love what you are doing.

"And believe in what you are doing.

"Yes," he said, "it's just that simple."

Now let's look into this advice a little more closely.

KNOW WHAT YOU ARE DOING

First, know what you are doing. There is no substitute for knowledge.

In our approach to knowledge we must realize that preparation is a constant process with no ending. It must be forever moving, never static. School is never out for the person who really wants to succeed. There is no saturation point. All economic research centers agree that because of the rapidly changing phases of our economy, the average person in any line of endeavor today, regardless of his particular field, must be retrained at least four times during his lifetime. Think of this:

What was not only right, but even plausible yesterday, is questionable today and might even be wrong tomorrow.

It is somewhat disenchanting, I know, to find that just as we learn one role in life we are suddenly called upon to play an entirely new part, unrehearsed, as the drama of life must go on either with us, or without us.

Knowledge is accumulating so fast and methods of doing things improving so rapidly that a person today must run to stand still.

Up to 1900 it was said that the accumulation of knowledge doubled every century. At the end of World War II, knowledge doubled every twenty-five years. Today all research centers tell us that the volume of knowledge in existence doubles every five years. Where does that leave the person today who thinks he can stand still and survive?

TRUE SUCCESS IS A JOURNEY, NOT A DESTINATION

The constant demands of readjustment offer a challenge today that never existed before. No longer is preparation something that can be put in a drawer and forgotten about. Success itself has taken on a new definition. It might even be termed today as the constant and continuing preparation of ourselves to meet the constant and continuing changes of our economic system. Yes, success today is a journey, and not a destination.

Furthermore, in making this trip the important thing is that we must be constantly moving forward — yes, the progressive realization of a predetermined goal. And our growth should never end. Any person who selects a goal in life which can be fully achieved, has already defined his own limitations. When we cease to grow, we begin to die.

HORIZONS OF CHANGE

One of the confusing mysteries to a child who travels along any road is that he cannot ever catch up with the horizon. None of us today can ever catch up with the horizons of change. We can only move in their direction. I am sure it is a blessing that our reach does exceed our grasp. If our ambitions in life can be fully reached, then we have not hitched our wagon to a star. We would do a great injustice to anyone if we painted the journey as being a path of roses. It is a pilgrim's road, full of obstacles and sacrifices. The only promise we can make is that if a person is willing to brave the hazards of the road, he will grow strong in the journey and keep pace with changing times.

I am sure you agree with me that regardless of how well qualified a person may be to meet the rigors of life today, if he is lulled into a sense of false security in feeling that he needs no additional preparation for the future, that his journey can ever be ended, soon he will find that he is lost in the frustrations of medieval thinking.

We have heard it said many times that there is nothing in life as powerful as an idea whose time has arrived — knowledge that is timely. If ideas are to be current and if knowledge is to be up to date, they must be forever moving, never static.

And so, first and foremost, we must embrace the principle that in order to be knowledgeable in these changing times we must pursue a constant program of self-improvement, a never-ending journey into new fields of knowledge and learning.

A DAY OF SPECIALIZATION

Because of the rapidly accumulating volume of knowledge today, it is becoming increasingly important to specialize in some business, industry or profession. There is no escape. This, of course, doesn't mean that an individual should not be well informed in the broad fundamentals and generalities. But it does mean that in addition to this he should to some extent be particularly knowledgeable in some aspect of his endeavors.

A rather frustrated individual the other day said, "Since we must know more and more about less and less, I guess this also means we must know less and less about more and more, which also means, pretty soon we are going to know everything about nothing and nothing about everything."

JUST HOW SPECIALIZED ARE WE?

Two fellows were talking the other day and one said, "Do you know, things are getting so specialized today that the National Biscuit Company even has a Vice-President in Charge of Fig Newtons."

The other said, "I don't believe it."

"I'll bet you," said the first.

So they put up the money and then proceeded to call the National Biscuit Company.

One said, "I want to speak to the Vice-President in Charge of Fig Newtons."

The answer came back, "Packaged or loose?"

The president of one of the largest rubber companies was recently making a speech. After he finished, the chairman opened the meeting for questions. A young man in the front row said, "Would it be too personal if I asked you how you got to be president of this big company?"

"Not at all," was the president's reply, "I was working in a filling station and not making much progress. One day I read that if a person wanted to get ahead he must know all there was to know about his particular product.

"So, on one of my vacations I went back to the home office and watched them make rubber tires. I'd watch them put in the nylon cords. On one vacation I went to Africa to watch them plant the rubber trees and even extract the base of crude rubber.

"So that when I talked about my product, I didn't say, 'this is what I'm told,' or 'this is what I read,' or 'this is what I think.' No, I said, 'this is what I know. I was there. I watched them put those nylon cords in to make the finest tire ever made, to protect your family against blow-outs. I watched them extract that crude rubber to make the finest tire in the world.'"

He then continued, "There is no force in the world that has a greater impact than the statement of a knowledgeable person fortified by confidence and experience."

A man who knows, and knows he knows, can speak with authority that has no comparison. The world makes way for a man who knows what he's doing.

ONLY ONE WEALTH ON THIS EARTH

Lincoln once said, "The older I get the more I realize that there is but one wealth, one security, on this earth and that is found in the ability of a person to perform a task well." But he didn't stop there. He went on to say, "And first and foremost this ability must start with knowledge."

A superficial knowledge is not enough. It must be a knowledge capable of analyzing a situation quickly and making an immediate decision.

A quarterback in the closing moments of an important game called the wrong signal. A pass was intercepted and the game and conference championship were lost. That was on a Saturday. By Tuesday afternoon he had courage enough to venture out and be seen. He had to go out and get a haircut.

The barber, after a long silence, said, "I've been studying and thinking about that play you called last Saturday ever since you called it, and you know, if I had been in your shoes I don't believe I would have called it."

The quarterback without changing expression said, "No, and if I'd had until Tuesday afternoon to think about it, I wouldn't have either."

In this modern competitive and fast moving economy of today we often don't have time to think things over and give the careful consideration to each situation which we would desire.

But still, I repeat, a superficial knowledge is not enough. Furthermore, a person who tries to substitute "gimmicks and gadgets and gizmos" for knowledge usually finds that it all boomerangs on him — he meets himself coming around the corner.

Such an attempt reminds one of the head hunter who bought himself a new boomerang. Then he spent the rest of life trying to throw the old one away.

I feel very sorry for anyone who thinks it's possible to substitute pull or personality or any other quality for fundamental knowledge.

Yes, let's remember the sound advice of Will Rogers. If we are to be successful we must first know what we are doing.

LOVE WHAT YOU ARE DOING

But as we stated earlier in this book, knowledge, important as it is, is not enough to insure success in our complex society today. We have often heard it said, "A merely well-informed man is the most useless bore on earth."

What was Will Rogers' next statement?

Not only know what you are doing, but love what you are doing.

What are we working for? Do we love our work or are we working for money alone? If it's for money alone we are underpaid, regardless of what we are making—furthermore, that's all we shall be working for as long as we live.

Everybody loves to do business with an optimist. We can only be an optimist if we love what we are doing.

Nothing takes a greater toll on us than to be around a pessimist — a person always finding fault and criticizing others. We've all seen the type. He has mental B.O. He's a one man grievance committee, always in session. He criticises everyone and everything. You ask him how is business and he says, "Well, I made a sale Monday. I didn't sell anything Tuesday. Wednesday the deal I made Monday fell through — so, I guess Tuesday was really my best day."

I was recently in Boston attending a convention. I was kicked out of the hotel after two days. I thought I had a three day reservation.

As the elevator came down it stopped at the seventh floor, but nothing happened. I was irritated and in a hurry to catch an early plane and said, "Come on in."

Nothing happened.

Again I said firmly, "Come in; let's get the show on the road."

Still nothing happened.

Finally, in a loud voice, I said, "Come on in — let's go. I'll be left."

At that moment a fine looking man with a white cane, completely blind, stepped in cautiously feeling his way along.

I felt awful. I had to say something, so I cleared my throat and said, "How are you today?"

He smiled and said, "Grateful, my friend, grateful."

I couldn't say a thing—I was choked up. Any impatience or worry I had, simply shrivelled into nothingness.

Here was a man blessing the darkness while I was cursing the light. I couldn't have cared less whether I caught that plane. I found myself that night in my prayers asking that some day I might see as well as that person.

Actually, each morning when we wake up if we don't find our names listed in the obituary column we should be so grateful that we are happy all day.

We can say something nice about every person or subject involved in a conversation. If not, we can at least remain silent. Nothing is *all* wrong.

Someone said that even the Black Hole of Calcutta was easy to heat.

Down in Mississippi we would say that Prohibition was horrible but that it was better than no whiskey at all.

I heard a man's name brought up the other day and someone lowered his voice and said, "Why, that fellow's a confirmed alcoholic."

The other person present said, "Well, at least, he ain't no quitter."

Let's follow Will Rogers' advice; let's constantly seek a little larger slice out of life, a few more acres of the Garden of Eden. Let's look for the happier things of existence. The great Will Rogers had the reputation of never criticizing. Why? Because he never met a man he didn't like.

BELIEVE IN WHAT YOU ARE DOING

Yes, Will Rogers said, "Know what you are doing—love what you are doing."

But he didn't stop there. He went further and said, "Believe in what you are doing."

I heard of a man who telephoned his friend and said, "Jake, I'm having a little informal birthday party tomorrow night and I want you to come to it. Come just as you are, don't stand on any ceremony. Just come right on up to the door and ring the door bell with your elbow and come right in."

The fellow said, "Well, that's all fine and good, but why my elbow?" His friend said, "Jake, maybe you didn't understand. It's my birthday. You are not coming empty handed, are you?"

Above all else, after you finish this book I don't want you to be empty handed. If you feel amused at a few anecdotes, if you are emotionally stirred or even mentally stimulated, that's not enough.

THE ULTIMATE IN HUMAN PERSUASION

In order that you will not be empty handed I shall give you in the next few sentences the greatest principle of human persuasion that exists. There is nothing which is even a close second. If there is anything in this book that is worth remembering it is this:

> *People are persuaded more by the depth of your conviction than by the height of your logic — more by your own enthusiasm than any proof you can offer.*

If I could describe the art of persuasion in one sentence it would be this and I know I would be right: Persuasion is converting people—no, not to our way of thinking but to our way of feeling and believing. And if a person's belief is sincere enough and deep enough he is a walking climate of positive acceptance. He has an obsession that cannot be denied.

The most persuasive person in the world is the man who has a fanatical belief in an idea, a product or a service. The one common denominator of all great men in history is that they believed in what they were doing. If we could choose but one lantern to guide our footsteps over the perilous quicksands of the future it should be the guiding light of dedication.

It has been said that words are the fingers that mold the mind of man. Words, however, can be refused. But a positive attitude that springs from a sincere belief cannot.

YOU MUST FIRST BELIEVE IN THE IDEA YOURSELF

I've heard people say in effect, "Do you believe in clairvoyance, telepathy, or psychoprediction? It's a strange thing, I knew that person was going to accept my idea the moment I walked in. Do you think I could have received thought transference?"

The answer is too obvious to need elaboration. The person presenting the idea had already made the big sale. He had bought the idea himself so completely that he was practically hypnotic in his persuasive powers.

On the other hand, I have heard a person say, "I can't explain it but I knew that fellow was not going to accept my idea even before I opened my mouth."

Of course he wasn't. The person presenting the idea didn't believe in it and he radiated this lack of belief. He was simply admitting that he had no enthusiasm for the idea and consequently he couldn't project any enthusiasm.

Yes, I repeat, the world is a looking glass and gives back to every person a reflection of his own thoughts, beliefs and enthusiasm.

I have a picture at home that a friend painted for me. It's a picture of an old tramp sitting on a park bench. He has holes in his shoes, his knees are out and he needs a shave. His hair looks as though it had been combed with an eggbeater and he's chewing a straw. A Rolls Royce goes by driven by a chauffeur, carrying a man in a tall silk hat.

The tramp looks at it lazily and philosophically says, "There, except for me, go I."

DON'T CHAIN YOURSELF TO MEDIOCRITY

The only chains and shackles that prevent any of us from realizing our life's dreams are those we ourselves forge in the fires of doubt and hammer out on the anvil of lack of belief in what we say or do.

Will Rogers, bless his great heart, said:

"KNOW WHAT YOU ARE DOING

"LOVE WHAT YOU ARE DOING

"BELIEVE IN WHAT YOU ARE DOING"

Where can we find any directional compass in life better than this?

I know of no qualities that can be a better formula to follow — a safer directional compass — than these three great directives of Will Rogers. Study them carefully and have faith in their guiding quality. They can lead only to success.

HUMAN ENGINEERING IS
A TICKET TO ANYWHERE

As set forth in the preface of this book, one of the mysteries of mankind is that we find 20 percent of the people in practically every line of endeavor responsible for 80 percent of the constructive activities of this life and the other 80 percent responsible for the remaining 20 percent.

Why are some people creators of circumstances and others, with equal opportunity, only creatures of circumstances? Why do things happen to some people and why is it that others happen to things?

I hope this book will assist you in understanding this great mystery of life. I hope you will better realize why the human engineer finds people his opportunity rather than his problem — why, to him, life is not mystery but magic, logic and not luck.

LET'S HAVE EMPATHY

Every treatise on the subject of communication today, whether it be a book, article or record, carries something about that new plateau of understanding called empathy. I suppose its simplest meaning is an assurance that I am writing and that you are reading about the same thing — that we are in tune, that we are on the same wave length.

There is quite a difference between sympathy and empathy. For instance, let's assume that you and I are out in the ocean fishing. If you should get seasick and I said "I am sorry," that's only sympathy, but if I became green too, that would be empathy.

I once heard of a very fine example of empathy. A plumber wrote the Department of Measurements in Washington and asked the simple question, "Is it safe to put hydrochloric acid in pipe?"

He received a letter in reply as follows: "The efficacy of the method is undeniable but the precipitate corrosive residue is incompatible and not conducive to metallic permanence."

The plumber studied the letter for a long time and finally wrote back, "I don't understand — all I want to know is whether I can put hydrochloric acid in pipe?"

Finally after the letter was kicked around from desk to desk it reached someone who had complete empathy with the plumber. He wrote back and said, "Don't do it, Mac, it'll eat hell out of the pipe."

I hope you and I at this point in this book are having complete empathy. I hope I am writing and you are reading about the same thing.

LET'S TAKE AN IMAGINARY JOURNEY

One Saturday night a businessman found himself in a little town in the territory he served. His car needed repairs and he couldn't drive to his home town.

The streets were bare; there was no entertainment to be found. Very bored and somewhat cynical he walked up to a stranger on Main Street and sarcastically asked, "What is this town noted for anyway?"

The local member of the Chamber of Commerce straightened himself up and proudly said, "My friend, you can start from this town and go anywhere in the world you want to go."

I'm not sure that he was not telling the stranger off, but in any event it gives me a cue to invite you to take a little imaginary journey with me. Imagine that you have a little card in front of you. I suppose a card is made up of pulp, rags or wood and a few chemicals, but if you will just for a few minutes fill in this card mentally with me, I'll guarantee it can take you anywhere in the world you want to go — that is, if you really want to make the trip.

If you sincerely and voluntarily fill it out, it can be a ticket to take you anywhere in life; it can be a magic carpet that will take you to the great city of your dreams, aspirations and ambitions; it can be a key to open the door to the miracle of life with its wondrous possibilities. All of this is possible, however, only if you really want to make the trip.

Now let's examine this card and fill it out carefully.

FIRST — WHAT IS OUR DESTINATION?

What is the first thing we see on any ticket? Yes, it's our destination, isn't it? Where do we really want to go in life?

Some people just don't want to go anywhere. They are bogged down in complacency and are satisfied to remain there. About all we can say for these people is that we hope they vegetate silently, unobtrusively and don't affect the lives of those around them.

JUST A SHORT TRIP

Then we have those people who want to take just a little trip, they don't want to go very far. They want to hurry back to status quo. They have built-in limitations. They want a life of quiet desperation. They flit from mediocrity to mediocrity with enthusiasm and optimism.

As for this second group of people, all we can say is that they were born in inertia and had a relapse. They don't even burn the candle at one end. They are suffering from that scientific disease that's known in technical circles as laziness.

THEY ADVISE OTHERS IN THEIR TRAVELS

Also we have those people who don't want to take the trip, but they pose as experts on criticizing the travels of others. It's a "dog in the manger" situation. They are like the man who didn't kiss his wife for 30 years and finally shot the guy who did. They don't want to take the trip and they don't want anyone else to take the trip either.

The only thing we can say about these critics is that they were born in the objective case and have been walking around in the subjunctive mood ever since.

AS FAR AS THE TICKET WILL TAKE THEM

Finally, we have those people who want to go as far as the ticket will take them. They truly have the gift of dissatisfaction and divine discontent. They have hitched their hearts to a task they love—their souls are blazing with purpose and they know where they want to go.

These people are not afraid to reach for the stars. They know that even should they miss they'll at least not come up with a handful of mud. They'd rather shoot at something and miss than shoot at nothing and hit. They're ever conscious of the fact that there is no such thing as a trip without a destination, no such thing as success without a purpose. Ever mindful are they that obstacles are only those things we see when we take our eyes off our goal. Long ago they learned that people do not fail in this life because they plan to fail—they fail because they fail to plan.

YOUR DESTINATION MUST BE SPECIFIC

Nothing clutters up the landscape of understanding and congeals confusion as do generalities. Specifics alone give a directional compass to life.

Do you really have a specific goal in life? What is it? Is it that you want to put your kids through college? Is it to be head of your firm—president of your company? You must have something specific you desire. If your desire is great enough, this one quality brings into focus all the other qualities within you which enable you to accomplish your specific goal.

I shall state a tragic fact. In our country, the greatest country in the world, if I went out and stopped the next two dozen people on the street, there would not be six who could recite a specific desire which governs their lives. And I am afraid there wouldn't be a dozen who could tell with certainty just why they went to work this morning.

And so the first thing we must insert in our ticket is our destination. Without this there is no trip at all. Just as it is impossible to come back from some places we have never been, it is altogether preposterous even to suppose that we can arrive anywhere without a place to go.

Yes, we must have a destination.

SECOND — WHAT IS OUR TIME SCHEDULE?

What's the next thing we see on any ticket? It's the time schedule. When do we want to go? And more important still, when do we want to arrive at our destination? Do we want to go now, from this very room, today—this moment? Or do we want to join those disenchanted people who are always putting something off until tomorrow and consequently never take the trip?

One of the unhappy circumstances of this life is that the world is full of well-meaning but misguided people who want to prepare for the future. In fact, they periodically vow emphatically that they want success enough to do something about it, and yet somehow they never get around to it. How many of these people do you know who are always about ready to commence to begin to start to do something pretty soon.

Unless you decide to go now, I guarantee you'll never take the journey. Why? I'll tell you why. There is no tomorrow. Yesterday does not exist. We live only today, right now, this very hour. Our only existence is the present.

THE MAGIC AND MIRACLE OF TIME

Does time really have a meaning to us? Each day we have the opportunity to watch the magic and miracle of time. Time—life's most priceless tool, that which cannot be weighed in the balance or tested in the crucible. But we know it is the only ingredient that we use to transform our dreams into realities and our hopes into success.

A NEW GIFT EACH DAY

Did it ever occur to us also that God in His infinite wisdom gives time to us in such small doses that we can't too easily squander it? Every morning, when I wake up, my pocketbook is magically filled with 24 hours of this precious, priceless substance we call time. And when tomorrow comes and I know that I have given up a whole day of my life for it, I want it to be for something that's good, not bad, some gain, not loss — something I can be proud of. And yet, Nature is so forgiving. Even if I waste it, "each night I burn the records of the day. At sunrise every soul is born again." Again I wake up — 24 more of those non-refundable fragments of eternity that are magically in my pocketbook — just as valuable and unused as if I had not thrown the others away.

Did you ever hear a person say, "I just don't have time." What he is really saying is that there are other things more important to him. We all have a lot of time. We have all the time there is. The hands of the clock go around at the same rate of speed for everyone of us. The main thing is that sometimes we do not put importance on those things that are important. We give inconsequential matters disproportionate importance. Yes, we major in the minors and we minor in the majors.

92

THE TRIP IS NOW OR NEVER

Just how valuable is your time to you? Can you afford not to start the trip today? Our time is too valuable to waste, and since we know there is no tomorrow, then unless we fill in today's date on our ticket, I am afraid that next week, next month, next year, ten years from now, honest as may be our intentions, we shall find ourselves in the wilderness of procrastination, still responding to the siren songs of complacency.

Why can't we realize that there is no other way except by starting today? Don't we feel honestly that we are worth the investment?

STARTING NOW IS OUR ONLY INSURANCE

Most people would not drive their car from the garage unless it were fully covered by insurance. Practically everyone has insurance on his house. Very few people would dare to subject themselves to the dangers of everyday living without life insurance.

And yet insurance-minded as these people may be, many of them are not insuring their futures against constant changes by starting NOW to prepare themselves to cope with these changes.

The world owes us nothing, but we owe ourselves, our loved ones and the entire world the duty to develop our God-given qualities to the ultimate. It is a great challenge and not an easy one to meet. But it is up to us and us alone to make our dreams come true, our plans come alive.

And so, look at your ticket again. Let's make the date today—this very moment. It is the only way that we can be sure that we shall get our just share of the tasks and rewards of this life. If we don't start now, we shall never reach the great city of our ambitions and aspirations.

THIRD — WHAT IS OUR ROUTE?

What's next on our ticket? It's the route, isn't it?

Let's not be seduced by the temptation to try the easy paths of life. Some people say that the great focal point of life is where the two highways of preparation and opportunity cross. Others call it luck. I won't argue the point but this I do know. Strength always flows from adversity. Troubles, trials, and sacrifices have always constituted the fertile soil for growth. If you will take time carefully to review your life, you, as does everyone else, will realize that you make your greatest progress in life during times of discouragement and challenge. You will find that the lasting qualities of life are usually forged on the anvil of disappointment.

While no one seeks hardships, yet we know that they can't be avoided along the highway leading to success. Our only choice is to meet them squarely and rise above them. The road will never be easier — it is up to us to become stronger.

AN OPTIMISTIC ROUTE

Please be sure also that you take an optimistic route. We read so much about positive thinking these days that we are tempted to be casual in considering its importance. But please never forget the sweet magic of a cheerful disposition. Everyone enjoys being around an optimist.

On the other hand a pessimist takes such a toll on us. I'd much prefer that a man steal my money than steal my optimism. The reason a pessimist is so dangerous is due to the law of emotional gravity. One pessimist can pull six optimists down with less effort than six optimists can lift up one pessimist.

Yes, we want to be kind and helpful to everyone possible, but to expose ourselves to a person with the smallpox of pessimism is a calculated risk too grave to take.

93

A ROUTE OF HAPPINESS

The next route is closely connected with the last one mentioned. We cannot be successful in our work or undertaking in life unless we enjoy what we are doing and feel a sense of fulfillment. Unless we are happy in what we are doing we are a job hazard, a professional malcontent.

Years ago I was attending a convention on salesmanship. There were six or eight small meetings going on simultaneously. One that attracted my attention was labeled "The Greatest Sale I Ever Made." I was intrigued and could hardly wait to get to the meeting. I was sure that the speaker would relate his experiences in difficult persuasion. I thought perhaps I would hear that a man ninety years old had bought a twenty-year endowment life insurance policy. Maybe, I felt, the speaker would relate the old cliché about selling two milking machines to a farmer with just one cow and then taking the cow in as a down payment.

What I really heard was this: "The greatest sale I ever made in my life was the day I finally bought what I was doing—the day I saw the big picture, the day I had the great concept, the great passion—yes, when I truly began believing in what I was doing."

THE ROUTE OF SERVICE

We can believe in what we are doing and feel a permanent sense of fulfillment only if we know we are rendering

■   ■   ■

a service to others. Any undertaking divorced from this feature has no lasting attraction. Never forget that service is the only rent we pay for the space we occupy while we are here on earth.

A person who desires to become rich should certainly not be criticized, provided he desires to become rich for the proper reason. There is certainly nothing wrong with a desire to prosper. We can do so much more for our loved ones and contribute so much more to the worth while programs in life if we are financially able. But if you are to be successful in such an undertaking you must never lose sight of this cardinal principle: *You can never become truly rich except by enriching the lives of others; you will never truly prosper unless you bring prosperity to others.*

So, in filling out our ticket let's not look for an easy route, but one that will make ourselves stronger. Also it should be an optimistic route and a happy route. And never lose sight of the fact that unless it is a route of service it will lead only up a blind alley. Man is so constituted that he must feel a sense of fulfillment if life is to have any permanent meaning. Some people feel that an undertaking must be monumental and world shaking to offer a challenge. This should not be. The size of the project is of minor importance—of major importance is the unselfish effort and dedication with which we tackle the job. Remember that any place of duty, however small, is a shrine wherein we can glorify our lives with the blessings of service.

FOURTH — ARE WE WILLING TO PAY THE PRICE?

And finally at the bottom of any ticket we see this—the PRICE.

So many of us want to take the trip, but how few of us are willing to pay the price of the ticket. All of us want to improve our circumstances but how few of us are first willing to make the sacrifices to improve ourselves. I get enthusiastic over the idea of building a greater future but do I have that same enthusiasm for the slow tedious task of building myself?

I shall tell you of an incident which changed my life and which also illustrates my point. This story is related in a former book of mine.*

I was attending a college in Greenville, South Carolina, called Furman University. A professor by the name of F. P. Gaines taught me English my freshman year. He later became president of Washington and Lee University.

Dr. Gaines called on us in alphabetical order. I can repeat the entire roll call even to this day. It was important to commit the roster to memory because if you always knew just when you would be called upon there was no need to prepare for recitation except about once each 2 months—at least that was my feeling during those green years of my life.

Furthermore, good sportsmanship demanded that if a person was sick, or absent for any other reason, he was duty bound to protect those students whose names followed his by notifying them in ample time to fortify themselves for recitation.

On a certain day when my name was fairly well up the list a very embarrassing situation presented itself. Raleigh and Riley didn't show up at class and neither one had pressed the panic button. I was unprepared, a rather normal condition under the circumstances. I had been over to a neighboring girls' college the night before to see the girl who is now the mother of my five kids.

Fortunately, however, Dr. Gaines, as he so often did, had departed from the subject of the day and was giving one of his little informal talks on some phase of personal development, which was consuming time. I have long ago forgotten the definition of a nominative predicate or the subjunctive mood. I sadly say that I am not sure I could even accurately parse a sentence. But I shall never forget some of the great inspirational ideas of life he gave us, nor will any who attended his classes ever cease to feel forever the impact of his great personality.

On this particular day Dr. Gaines had been discussing character. Finally he picked up his roster and I knew that I was to be called on next. I glanced up at the clock and suddenly realized that the dismissal bell would ring in five minutes.

Frantically, I blundered out as I grabbed a pen and looked for a piece of paper, "Dr. Gaines, could you give us a definition of character that we could write down?"

He looked at me and then looked up at the clock as I reddened, realizing how transparent my improvised scheme had turned out to be. But he was the essence of kindness and gentleness. He looked at me and smiled. He realized, of course, that I couldn't have cared less about the definition of character.

Dr. Gaines walked around the room in silence for about a minute with his hands behind him and his chin tilted slightly upward, which was a favorite pose of his. Finally he stopped in front of me, put his left hand on my shoulder and pointed his finger in my face.

"Young fellow," he said, "I'm not sure, but I am going to give you a definition that I want you to keep until you can find a better one."

That has been almost forty years ago and I have never heard one half as good.

"Character," he said slowly, "is the ability to carry out a good resolution long after the mood in which it was made has left you."

He continued, "Now I didn't say just the ability to carry out a good resolution. We all have our moments of supreme dedication—whether it be fidelity to a person or loyalty to an ideal. But how few of us carry out that resolution when the mood has left us and the tides of temptation come sweeping in.

"Tomorrow morning, you are going to have a test on the material we have covered over the past few days.

"Tonight you will perhaps decide that you are going to get up at six o'clock in the morning and study for this test. And actually you are going to get up in the morning—that is, tonight you are, because you are in the mood.

"But tomorrow morning when you stick your foot out and it touches the cold floor you don't have that mood any longer. I say character is that which you have within yourself to substitute for the mood which has left you. Character is that which causes you to exercise the self-discipline to get up anyway."

The bell had rung but none of us had heard it. We knew it must have rung because the room was invaded by the next class.

Those five minutes have burned brightly for me over the past forty years. I would not exchange them for any entire semester of my college career.

During those forty years, on many occasions I have committed myself to some project or assignment while I was in an enthusiastic mood. I was swept along with a compulsion at the time. After the mood was gone the picture was different. The task seemed drab and difficult and without glamour or attraction. The price to pay seemed too high. On such occasions I have tried to remember this definition of character—that which we have within us to substitute for the mood after it is gone.

It is so easy to accept all parts of the ticket except the price. This is where real character and self-discipline enter the picture.

95

DON'T SETTLE FOR A LIMITED TRIP

Let's look at our ticket again. If we have a definite destination, if we are willing to start now, if we do not look for the easy route but for one that will make us stronger, an optimistic route, a route of service, and finally, if we are willing to pay the price, then we can with certainty know that our little ticket can take us anywhere in life we want to go. I repeat that it can be a magic carpet that will take us to the great city of our dreams, our ambitions and our aspirations. Yes, it can be a key that will open the door to the miracle of life with its limitless possibilities.

This journey is certainly not an easy trip. But human engineering is not for little people with little minds. It's not for people who are afraid the sun won't rise tomorrow. It belongs only to those brave and courageous people who dare to dream, have faith and expect the best. If you really want to take the trip you must be willing to be baptized by immersion in some of the tougher aspects of life.

It was about two thousand years ago that a great Greek philosopher and mathematician, Archimedes, was asked if he could perform a certain task.

This is what he said: "Give me a lever that is long enough, give me a fulcrum that is strong enough and give me a place to stand, and singlehanded I'll move the world."

Our lever is our goal in life. Our fulcrum is our self-discipline and willingness to pay the price. Furthermore, we must stand upon the firm ground of dedication and belief in our pursuits and activities in this life. If we have these qualities we too can move the world.

Read and re-read this chapter over and over. It has tools of greatness you cannot afford to ignore. Practice its principles and resolve to start your trip today.

96

---

*The Cavett Robert Personal Development Course, Parker Publishing Company 1966.

WHAT MAKES JOE GO?

It is said that an egotist talks about himself, a bore talks about others, but a brilliant conversationalist talks to you about you.

I do not claim the distinction of being a brilliant conversationalist, but I do want to concentrate for a few minutes on YOU.

My approach is going to be in the form of a question. It is one of the oldest questions that ever confronted mankind. It was old when the big stones were floated down the Nile to build the Pyramids. It wasn't new when our country was founded. Even today it is the sixty-four dollar question in the fabric of our entire economic life.

This is the question: Two people wake up in the morning in the same city; they are engaged in the same type of endeavor; all day long they are exposed to the same opportunities, tasks and rewards of this life.

One comes home that night happy, optimistic and with a feeling of fulfilled accomplishment. The other comes home disenchanted, discouraged and with a feeling of frustration.

Why the difference? They saw the same people. They walked the same streets. They offered the same service. The hands of the clock went around no faster for one than for the other.

Why is one successful and the other not? Why does one fall into that 20 percent responsible for 80 percent of the results and the other find himself relegated to tragic mediocrity or even failure?

If we can give a satisfactory answer to this question, we shall in some measure answer one of the oldest questions which ever confronted man—as old as time itself.

In offering as a solution some of the human engineering principles, I would like to keep our approach in the form of a question. The question is this: "WHAT MAKES JOE GO? WHAT MAKES JOE A PRO while his colleague is a failure?"

LET'S ASK JOE

I am sure we can do no better in our search for an answer than ask Joe himself. Let's see what Joe has to say.

Joe says, "Just lucky, I guess."

Joe tells us he is successful because he is lucky. Now let's not be too quick in passing judgment on Joe. I am sure he is not trying to dodge the question. He perhaps has a point.

Joe says he wants to break the work LUCKY down and explain it to us. He asks us to sit as a jury and let him offer his evidence. He is emphatic, however, that we reserve our verdict until he has presented his entire case and all the evidence is in.

L STANDS FOR LOYALTY

Joe says L stands for loyalty. Yes, he says that he must be loyal to himself, to his company and to the public he serves.

But first of all Joe feels that he must be loyal to himself. Our first impression might be that this is a rather selfish order of importance, but Joe feels otherwise.

Joe claims that the word "JOE" perhaps has little meaning to other people. But to him it's the sweetest word in the English language. It means everything in the world. He's not an egotist, but he wants to protect that word because he knows that if he loses it, he has nothing. He knows that he cannot be loyal to anybody or anything until he is first loyal to himself.

Shakespeare tells us, "Who steals my purse steals trash; 'tis something, nothing; Twas mine, 'tis his, and has been slave to thousands; But he that filches from me my good name robs me of that which not enriches him, and makes me poor indeed."

Joe is resolved to preserve that name. He knows that there is a law of human engineering, an everlasting law that can never be repealed: *Public opinion is a poor tyrant compared to what a man thinks of himself.*

LOYAL TO COMPANY FOR WHICH HE WORKS

But Joe's loyalty doesn't stop with himself—it only begins there.

Joe is loyal to the company or the man for whom he works. He believes in Elbert Hubbard's statement, "If you work for a man, in heaven's name, work for him; speak well of him and stand by the institution he represents."

If you want to resign, then it is a different story. But as long as you work for a man or a company, give your very best.

LOYAL TO THE PUBLIC

Joe says we must be loyal to the public. He says that we must be a go-giver as well as a go-getter—that we can solve our own problems only through solving the problems of others.

Unless we try to do more than our share, more than is expected of us, it is a law of human nature that we end up doing less than our share, less than is expected of us. Joe says he has never yet found a statue erected to the man who stands by waiting to go through a revolving door on someone else's push.

Yes, Joe is loyal—he is loyal to himself, his company and the public he serves.

U STANDS FOR UNDERSTANDING

Joe says that the second letter in LUCKY, U, stands for UNDERSTANDING.

Joe is above all else a human engineer. He is not satisfied with just knowing WHAT a person does or even WHY he does it. Understanding in order to have any value or meaning must reveal to him HOW to cause a person to act in a predetermined manner.

As we have emphasized earlier in this book, the mastery of the third dimension, the HOW, is the most important quality in graduating into the 20 percent group responsible for 80 percent of the results. If a person ever forgets for one moment that above all else he is in the people business, if he fails to remember that knowledge or information which is not related to the problems of people is of no value, he is immediately lost in the complexities of academic theory—his productive roots are in sterile soil.

We've all heard of the surgeon who said to the young intern, "I can teach you within one hour, skillfully to remove an appendix. But it will take me four years to teach you how to cope with an emergency if something goes wrong." Yes, it would take only one hour for the WHAT, but four years for the third dimension, the HOW.

In all of our relationships with other people let's always be mindful of the fact that we are human engineers, that we are in the people business, that we must understand the three dimensions of human engineering—the WHAT, the WHY, and the HOW.

Joe knows that if he uses only the "mumbo jumbo" in his dealings with others, he will "corn-pone" a few people into decisions he desires, but he will never know their reasons for buying or refusing. Joe assures us that U is one of the most important letters in his word, LUCKY, which he claims is responsible for success.

C IS FOR CHARACTER

Now Joe is no evangelist, he runs no revival meetings, he does not criticize the actions of others. But Joe knows this. He knows that a man cannot communicate better, he cannot convince better, he cannot do anything better until he first learns to live better. He has always known that the whole man must be developed.

Joe is careful not to be critical. If his friends want to go down to Ptomaine Tavern, they can go down every night if they choose and drink until morning. Still he doesn't criticize.

One of Joe's friends says he goes down there for just one drink. But he says that when he has that first drink it makes him feel like a new man. Then he has to buy the new man a drink. Then they must exchange drinks. Finally, his friend says, by the time he gets through with the formality, the inside of his mouth tastes like a policeman's shoe and he can't work the next day.

Another of Joe's friends says he drinks only for medicinal purposes—he's sick of being sober.

Joe respects the opinions of others but he has the courage to live by his own.

K STANDS FOR KNOWLEDGE

And what does K stand for? Joe tells us that it stands for KNOWLEDGE.

We have heard of the little boy who went into the drug store and said, "Mister, can I use your telephone?"

"Sure, Johnny," was the answer.

Johnny dialed a number and said, "Hello, is this 266-2509? I want to apply for a job as a gardener. Oh! You have a gardener. Is he a good gardener? Is he doing a fine job? You have no plans to change? Well, thank you anyway."

As Johnny started out of the door, the storekeeper called him back and said, "Don't be discouraged son. That's a very commendable thing you are doing. You'll get a job, Johnny. Just keep trying."

"Who's looking for a job?" was Johnny's reply.

Rather surprised, the storekeeper said, "I am sure I heard you ask for a job as a gardener."

"Well, you see, it's this way," said Johnny rather embarrassed, "I'm the gardener — I'm just checking on myself to see how well I am doing."

How often do we play "mirror, mirror on the wall?" How often do we evaluate ourselves to make sure we are keeping pace with changing times?

Just as an experiment ask yourself this very moment what you are doing as a result of a planned program to be sure that you are more knowledgeable in your line of endeavor than you were three months ago. How many periodicals in your field do you read each month? How many books have you read during the past year that will help you in your present work?

Joe realizes that the acquisition of knowledge is a never ending process. Being a human engineer, however, Joe is constantly increasing his "people knowledge" as well as his "product knowledge."

Y STANDS FOR YOU

And finally, Joe knows that Y stands for YOU. Joe says that success comes in a "can" and not in a "can't." Joe knows that there is but one can opener and that is YOU.

This letter in LUCKY is the very essence of human engineering — the very heart of the human equation. Joe knows that just as a book can be no greater than the author, the picture no greater than the painter, the statue no greater than the sculptor, we cannot accomplish anything greater than that which we are. Just as a physical law does not permit water to rise above its source, there is a law of nature which does not let a man's success in life rise above those qualities which are a source of this success.

One of the tragedies of this life is that many people are so much more concerned about what they OWN than about what they ARE. They would prefer having something to being something.

Joe learned early in life that what he eventually would own is only going to be a by-product of what he eventually is to be. The law of indirection taught him that if he is to build any material wealth in life, he must first start building himself.

On the wall of Joe's office hangs a framed Chinese proverb:
"Give a man a fish and he will eat for a day. But teach him how to fish and you have satisfied his hunger for life."

GROW, THROUGH YOUR ADVERSITY

To build one's self in not an easy thing. It can't be done overnight. It's a conditioning process as well as a learning process. To prepare a person "knowledge-wise" and not condition him and develop him "people-wise" is preparing him for failure.

The development of YOU is difficult, but in the difficulty lies the opportunity. If human development were easy, then there would be less congestion at the bottom of the ladder and more at the top, which is certainly not the case today.

We grow only in the crucible of adversity. Every hardship, even every disappointment, should be the seed of a new opportunity. Did you ever analyze a little stream of water? It has no strength within itself. It is shallow and weak. But if we put a dam across it, this obstacle will cause the water to back up and get depth. This obstacle has caused the water to have strength and power. It can now generate power to drive a locomotive and it can turn the wheels of industry.

There is a law of human development similar to Parkinson's law of time. That law is this: A person's strength will grow and increase to any extent to enable him to perform the task at hand. If a person is not confronted with some great tribulation, some great challenge, Nature sees no need of wasting her resources and precious tools upon him. But if he is confronted with obstacles and resolves to overcome them, she will open up her storehouse of riches and permit him to choose whatever materials and tools necessary for him to arise to the occasion, and meet the challenge which confronts him.

Joe tells us that LUCKY not only ends with YOU but that in reality it is the determining factor of our whole existence.

And so in Joe's behalf I claim that he has proved his case to you as a jury.

LUCKY—loyalty, understanding, character, knowledge, and you—yes, the blending of these various ingredients will create something that may spell LUCKY in English. But I am sure that in the great universal language it spells SUCCESS.

102

EPILOGUE

104

A Note From the Author

On August 29, 1997, when Dad was getting out of bed in the morning, he tripped and fell, breaking his left hip. Mom called the paramedics, and Dad was taken to Phoenix Baptist Hospital, where it was determined that he would have an operation that evening. The operation was successful, and the family was relieved that Dad came through it without incident.

The following day, the physical therapist, as is routine after a hip operation, tried to get Dad to take some steps. He resisted walking. He also resisted eating. Because Dad knew he would be a semi-invalid for the rest of his life, it is the family's belief that he chose this as his time to go. Two weeks later, he was gone. He died of double pneumonia.

—Lee Robert

Before Daddy died, he was visited by many loved ones and friends. Among those were Naomi Rhode, a past president of the National Speakers Association, who afterward sent the following special letter to her NSA friends and "family."

—Lee Robert

Dear Friends,

I know that all of us are filled to overflowing with love for Cavett, Trudy and the whole Robert family at this very difficult time. And, much more important, our prayers are encompassing the family as we join with them in grief at their loss. I know we are all blessed with the joy of knowing Cavett and the awesome privilege of being part of his legacy. I feel compelled to share with you my experience of the last few days and to reflect on the privilege of God's timing and guidance in all of our lives.

Wanting to honor the difficulty and privacy of the days following Cavett's surgery, we did not visit the hospital other than through our love and prayers. However, knowing we were leaving for Toronto early Saturday morning, I really felt God's strong leading to visit Cavett on Friday evening. My husband Jim and I met Jim and Coreen Hennig and Ed Scannell at the hospital for a truly touching time surrounding this dear man we all loved so much.

Cavett knew us all. He was, I believe, touched and happy with our presence, but in much pain. I asked him if I could pray for him, and he said, "Oh, please . . . oh, please." I prayed and felt the gentle touch of our Father's presence comforting us and this dear friend. We all then prayed the Lord's Prayer together, and Cavett joined weakly and emotionally.

Coreen Hennig — with her precious, soft, angelic voice — sang one song beautifully. Then we all joined in — with trembling voices, filled with our own concerns, knowing of what was coming — on "Amazing Grace." I believe we were joined, truly, by a choir of angels' voices. (And I know that you all were there praying and singing with us. Thank you for your presence, my "family of NSA"!!)

Cavett's chin trembled with tenderness, he thanked us for making this club what it is — how humbly put! — and we all hugged him and said goodbye. I do not think there was one of us who did not know this would possibly be the very last time on this earth we would give him, and receive his, love. We then left to speak at the first Canadian Association of Professional Speakers meeting in Toronto.

Cavett is now part of that "grandstand of saints, cheering us on to glory." It is truly "the blessed hope" of our faith, and I celebrate that knowing and that faith in a heightened way as I wipe away the tears one more time while giving a tribute to Cavett and to this group that would never have existed without him. How grateful I am for that experience!

And yes, now I must thank you all again for your precious gift to me!! You will never know what it means to Naomi Rhode to have been given "the Cavett" by the Cavett Robert for the very last time in Anaheim, California, July 1997.

—Naomi Rhode

CAVETT ROBERT— MOTIVATIONAL SPEAKER

On Monday, September 15, 1997, at 1:03 p.m., with his family and friends surrounding him with love and support, Cavett Robert left this earth. On Wednesday, September 17, *The Arizona Republic* newspaper printed this obituary by Eric Searleman.

CAVETT ROBERT, MOTIVATIONAL SPEAKER

Cavett Robert, a professional motivational speaker and Founder and Chairman Emeritus of the National Speakers Association, died September 15. The Phoenix resident was 89.

Mr. Robert was born in Starkville, Mississippi. He received his Bachelor of Science degree from the University of Mississippi before earning his law degree from Washington and Lee University in Virginia. After practicing law in New York, he moved to Arizona in 1937 for health reasons. In Phoenix, he established himself as a successful lawyer and insurance and real estate salesman.

Beginning his career as a platform speaker in the early sixties, Mr. Robert was the recipient of numerous awards. In 1972 he was given the Golden Gavel Award by Toastmasters International, and a year later he was selected Speaker of the Year by the United Airlines and International Speakers Network. He was the author of several books as well as more than a dozen inspirational recordings.

In 1972, Mr. Robert founded the National Speakers Association, located in Tempe. "Robert has served as an inspiration both on an individual level and through his work with the speakers association," said one prominent NSA member. "Because of Robert, the speaking profession now has a code of ethics and set of rules that benefit everyone involved."

The memorial service, held on Saturday, September 20, was attended by approximately 500 people at Church of the Beatitudes in Phoenix, Arizona. It was an upbeat service, with several of Cavett's favorite Strauss waltzes playing as the attendees were seated in the large and beautiful church, with floor-to-ceiling stained-glass windows depicting religious figures as well as great men and women throughout history.

In addition to Cavett's best friends, John Hammond and Joe Larson, sharing humorous and poignant anecdotes about his life, Lee sang the song she had written for him (see next page).

THE LAMPLIGHTER

Every night when twilight comes, a man I'd like to know,
Comes to light the lanterns high when he walks on down the road.
My Papa is a banker man, and his Daddy was before,
but I want to be a lamplighter as I walk to heaven's door.

Oh, Mr. Lamplighter, take me by the hand,
I don't know just where you're going, but I know where you've been.
Please, Mr. Lamplighter, let me walk with you.
Show me how to show the way, with a light that shines so true.

Yes, he lights the way for those who walk a pilgrim's journey road,
'cause there are those that would turn back, a carryin' their load.
But dark to light, he fills the night and hope can build anew.
I want to be a lamplighter who lights the way for you.

Oh, Mr. Lamplighter, take me by the hand,
I don't know just where you're going, but I know where you've been.
Please, Mr. Lamplighter, let me walk with you.
Show me how to show the way, with words that speak so true.

And so I sit beside the window sill and I will wait,
To catch a glimpse of the lamplighter as he walks to heaven's gate.
When I grow up, I know just what it is I want to be,
A lamplighter who lights the light inside of you and me.

Oh, Mr. Lamplighter, take me by the hand.
I don't know just where you're going, but I know where you've been.
Please, Mr. Lamplighter, let me walk with you.
Show me how to show the way, with a heart that loves so true . . .
with words that speak so true . . .
with a light that shines so true.

The following eulogy was given by Cavett Robert Jr.

I humbly stand before you as the first-born son of a great man. I was privileged to be named after that great man, Cavett Robert, Sr. We are all saddened by the passing of my father, but he led a rich and full life, and I know he would want us to remember his almost 90 years in a positive light.

Originally educated as an attorney, my father had the gift of being able to surgically dissect any argument or issue from multiple directions. This was no more apparent than when he would recite his now-famous "Whiskey Story," where he denigrates the "firewater" as the scourge of the earth only to quickly reverse directions on the subject and extol the virtues of this "nectar of the gods."

Cavett Sr.'s contributions to public speaking and motivation are legendary, but what really was inspirational relates to the passion and enjoyment he derived from speaking. He used to say, "Know what you're doing, love what you're doing and believe in what you're doing." We call these pithy chunks of wisdom *Cavettisms*. When we saw Dad in his pajamas, with tape recorder in hand, working late into the night, we soon realized that he loved to speak! Those speeches were filled with strokes of brilliance and originality, but his true genius was his deep love and understanding of his fellow man. He enhanced our lexicon by crystallizing this concept into the term *human engineering*.

What more fitting honor than for the National Speakers Association to make its yearly Oscar the Cavett Award; that was always his golden moment!

113

You will hear and read more about the many lives Dad touched and influenced in his professional career, but I now want to focus on a more personal side of my father. He was one of the most unselfish and generous men I have ever had the privilege of knowing. This manifested itself not only toward his family but also on a local and global scale.

Some measure of a man is surely judged by the love of his family. One of the true romances I have had the plea-sure of witnessing is the love affair my father perpetuated with my mother — his wife, Trudy — whom he con-stantly reminded us was Miss South Carolina of 1929 and whom he affectionately called "True-bug." As she is truly a Southern Belle, he was certainly the gold standard for a Southern Gentleman!

All five of his children took diverse paths in their lives, but there was no diversity in their genuine love and respect for their father. It was not just his family who loved this great man; he was beloved by multitudes. He might have had the coldest feet this side of the Mississippi, but his heart was warm and big enough to love us back. Maybe this is why he found it almost effortless to be so unselfish and so generous.

I now live in Lafayette, California, with my wife, Sande, and Cavett Senior's two granddaughters, Wesley Anne and Ashley Cavett Robert. Cavett Sr. is also survived by his two grandsons, William Cavett (nicknamed "Skee") and Carter Saacke, Skee's wife Katrina and a great grandchild, Keiko Madison Saacke.

■   ■   ■

Near our home in Lafayette is a statuesque mountain that I am fond of bicycling to when I am feeling especially energetic. One section of that mountain has a mixture of shrubbery that smells identical — it's almost a déjà vu — to a place near Phoenix where Dad used to take me dove hunting. I tell you this because that section of the Lafayette mountain always reminds me of those happy days when my father would take me out of school to go hunting or partake in other adventurous explorations.

A young boy blessed to hear his father's exciting stories, to share in the gustatory delight he derived from pecan pie and cold watermelon purchased at a roadside stand, to be introduced to hot mineral baths and massages at Buckhorn, to ride to the drive-in theater to see a double-feature shoot-'em-up Western, to be flown in his father's Piper Cub airplane to his favorite fishing spots and later to share a good cigar and exchange embellished stories with this remarkable man. He was more than a good father — he was my good friend.

And what a sense of humor! I remember his jokes and stories not for their humorous content, but for the sheer joy and infectious laughter he derived from telling them. It seemed that he laughed harder the more he repeated a joke. The stories seemed to always have a deeper meaning or a hidden message. For example, to say he spoiled his children is a rash understatement. In this context, he loved to tell the joke about the father who would constantly carry his adolescent son to school. Finally, someone asked the father, "Can't your son walk?" And the father replied, "Yes . . . but thank the Lord, he'll never have to!"

Another Cavettism is that "Service is the only rent we pay for the space we occupy while we're on this earth." The great landlord in the sky certainly was paid overtime for Cavett Senior's rent on this earth, and his family and community benefited immeasurably from that service. Uncompensated contributions were standard operating procedure for this noble soul!

Many of us have been profoundly influenced by this great man. Perhaps the greatest individual influence on my father's character was that of his mother, Hal. If there are any genetic doubters out there, they never met Cavett Senior's mother, Hallie Cavett Robert. She had the same charm, charisma and lovability that Dad possessed, and my father adored her beyond measure. I believe it was Hal who taught Dad to refer to his family as "The Proud House of Robert."

Dad used to say, "Life is a journey, not a destination!" Well, The Proud House of Robert is certainly very proud of Cavett Senior's journey. His destination now transcends to a higher level, where he will experience the warm and loving embrace of his mother, Hal, and his beautiful daughter, JoAnn.

We love you, Dad, and we thank you for letting us be part of your magic.

■   ■   ■

On Wednesday, September 17, two days after my dad passed away, I had a dream. In my dreamy state, I heard the telephone ring. When I answered it, still in my dream, it was my dad's voice. "Hello, dahhhlin," my Dad said in that love-filled Southern voice of his. "Daddy, is that you?" I asked. My dad communicated to me that he was just a "call away" . . . that he was there whenever I needed him. I might not be able to see him, but he was there for me, would always come when I called and would be in the front row at my presentations whenever I wanted. It may have been a dream, but for me it was real, and I felt very reassured. I believe for all of us he loved and mentored, he is just a "call away."

I would like to end with a toast Dad often gave at the end of his speeches.

May the hinges of friendship never rust,
may the wings of love never lose a feather,
and may this sacred circle of love grow deeper and stronger
each year, and not be broken as long as we live.
Because they tell me that a bell is not a bell until we ring it,
a song is not a song until we sing it,
love was not put in our hearts to stay,
love is only love when we give it away.
So here's to those we love, and here's to those who love us,
and here's to those we love who love those who love us!
So let's keep this a loving circle of friendship and never forget
that life is our greatest gift, and living nobly, our finest art.
And what we can do we oughta do, and what we oughta do we can do,
and what we can do and oughta do, I know by the grace of God we will do.
Good luck . . . God bless . . . I love every one of you.

REFLECTIONS
ON
CAVETT

NSA PRESIDENTS

1973–75	Bill Gove, CSP, CPAE		1986–87	Jim Tunney, EdD, CSP, CPAE
1975–76	Carl Winters, DD, CPAE (deceased)		1987–88	D. John Hammond
1976–77	Don Hutson, CSP, CPAE		1988–89	Jim Cathcart, CSP, CPAE
1977–78	Joe Larson, CSP		1989–90	Jerry Simmons, JD, CSP
1978–79	Ira M. Hayes, CPAE (deceased)		1990–91	Thomas J. Winninger, CSP, CPAE
1979–80	Ty Boyd, CSP, CPAE		1991–92	Edward E. Scannell, CSP
1980–81	D. Michael Frank, CSP, CPAE		1992–93	Al Walker, CSP, CPAE
1981–82	Don Thoren, CPAE		1993–94	Naomi Rhode, CSP, CPAE
1982–83	Nido R. Qubein, CSP, CPAE		1994–95	Michael P. McKinley, CSP, CPAE
1983–84	Robert H. Henry, CSP, CPAE		1995–96	James F. Hennig, PhD, CSP, CPAE
1984–85	Patricia Fripp, CSP, CPAE		1996–97	Patricia Ball, CSP, CPAE
1985–86	Jeanne Robertson, CSP, CPAE		1997–Present	Glenna Salsbury, CSP, CPAE

CAVETT AWARD RECIPIENTS

1979   Cavett Robert, CSP, CPAE (deceased)

1980   Bill Gove, CSP, CPAE

1981   Dave Yoho, CPAE

1982   Ty Boyd, CSP, CPAE

1983   Joe Larson, CSP

1984   Ira M. Hayes, CPAE (deceased)

1985   Nido R. Qubein, CSP, CPAE

1986   Don Hutson, CSP, CPAE

1987   James "Doc" Blakely, CSP, CPAE

1988   Robert H. Henry, CSP, CPAE

1989   Jeanne Robertson, CSP, CPAE

1990   D. Michael Frank, CSP, CPAE

1991   Rosita Perez, CPAE

1992   D. John Hammond

1993   Jim Cathcart, CSP, CPAE

1994   George L. Morrisey, CSP, CPAE

1995   Thomas J. Winninger, CSP, CPAE

1996   Patricia Fripp, CSP, CPAE

1997   Naomi Rhode, CSP, CPAE

The following pages feature the reflections of those NSA past presidents and Cavett Award recipients who generously shared their remembrances of Cavett for this book.

ONE OF A KIND

We talk about the importance of being unique in the speaking profession. That is certainly a word that fit Cavett Robert. He was one of a kind. If every person in the world would emulate the spirit of Cavett, what a magnificent place this would be!

I knew Cavett from the time I joined NSA in 1977. Always the epitome of the Southern gentleman, he used to call me Wonder Woman. This was during the era of the TV show *Wonder Woman,* starring Linda Carter. I bore a slight resemblance to her, and Cavett flattered me by noticing that resemblance.

Cavett was an encourager of the first order, seeing in people possibilities that even they had not yet realized. When I was elected to my beginning term on the NSA board of directors, Cavett was among the first to congratulate me. He commented, "You are just the kind of board member we need. I can't wait until you're president of NSA!" At that time, being NSA president was the furthest thing from my mind. But Cavett kept encouraging me until I developed enough confidence that I thought, "Yes, I can do that!"

When I was elected vice president by the NSA board, it was only a matter of time before I would attain the presidency. Cavett's prophesy would become a reality in July 1996. But he was getting on in years and becoming frail; I was worried about his health. I said to him, "Cavett, you must be there for the national convention while I'm president . . . after all, you are largely responsible." He commented, "Oh, I'll be there . . . I wouldn't miss it! You can count on me!" And sure enough, for the highlight of my life, at the NSA 1997 summer convention in Anaheim, Cavett was in his seat in the front row. We honored him at that convention with a magnificent quilt designed and made by Kathy Lamancusa.

That was the last time I saw Cavett. During the workshops earlier this year, I looked at the empty front-row seat where he had always sat. I miss you, Cavett. There will never be another like you. You were indeed one of a kind!

121

—PATRICIA BALL

THE SPEAKER'S PERFECT ROLE MODEL

It would be easy enough to say what a selfless, caring, giving man was Cavett Robert. Everybody who knew him knows that, so as a humorist, I would rather concentrate on his grand sense of humor and how it impacted me.

Cavett could not only tell a good story in a funny way, but he could take a joke at his own expense. On several occasions, I poked a little good-natured fun at him by doing impressions of him at NSA meetings . . . the way he said "oith" for earth and "boith" for birth in his Mississippi drawl, and I exaggerated his seemingly already exaggerated body language. He and Trudy always laughed the loudest, and I could tell from their convulsions that their mirth was genuine. Afterwards, Cavett was always the "foist" to tell me I was great and without a doubt the best humorist he had ever "hoid." Of course, this compliment was tempered by the remark made by some wag: "Yeah . . . Cavett thinks everybody he hears is the greatest in the world." To paraphrase Will Rogers, whom Cavett had met and was fond of quoting, "He never heard a speaker he didn't like."

One of the earliest speeches I remember Cavett giving was a session at NSA where he was telling "war stories" about the circuit — about hecklers, in particular. He had experienced enough of them that he had developed a few stock remarks to help him through difficult encounters. One story made me aware of how important it is not to take yourself too seriously as a gifted orator and imbedded in my mind the need to present oneself as humble and human. It was the kind of self-deprecating humor that endeared Cavett to all and a lesson that influenced me in a positive way to follow similar guidelines.

Cavett was halfway into a talk, sharing his usual witty stories and motivational anecdotes, whipping himself into a frenzy more than usual for this tough audience. A man raised his hand as if to ask a question, although questions are not customary during keynote presentations. Politely, the gentleman from Mississippi stopped and, in his rapid-fire way, asked if the man had a problem, needed to be excused or wanted to ask a question. The man replied, "I want to tell a story." Cavett shot back, "Well, sir, I want to hear your story, and when I have finished my speech, I want you to meet me in the back of the room, and I will be most happy to give you my undivided attention." Usually, this type of response takes care of such a situation without further interruption.

Cavett continued his speech with humor and motivation. The fellow raised his hand again. "I still want to tell my story," he replied. Stunned at the fellow's persistence, Cavett said, "Well, then, come on up here and tell it. I'll trade places with you." To quote Cavett's account of the scenario: "The guy started in to telling a funny story, and by gosh, it was goooood. In fact, it was better than anything I had been telling. When he sat down to thunderous applause, I finished up quickly and got the heck out of theah."

We all laughed uproariously, but the message that came through will stay with me for as long as I have memories of Cavett. Here was the role model of perfection in our business admitting that: 1) he didn't always knock 'em dead in Kankakee, 2) even the best professionals have something to learn from amateurs and 3) stressfully painful events separated by time and introspection equal humor that an audience can appreciate because the retelling of them allows the audience to feel superior, at least for a moment, to the big shot up front.

The first recipient of his namesake award, Cavett used this cherished, almost revered bronze of himself in a way that's indicative of his own humility. Every morning in Arizona, he'd walk out to the front yard to pick up the daily paper, which was encircled by a rubber band. On his way back inside, he'd pass his bronze image, sculpted in the famous Robert pose — right hand raised, index finger pointing upward at a 45-degree angle, left hand outstretched. The right hand was at just the right angle for the great orator to use it as a depository for hundreds of rubber bands from his daily papers.

Cavett left us with his head on straight and his funny bone intact.

—DOC BLAKELY

THE DREAM MERCHANT

He was one of a kind by many measures. Born in Mississippi. Educated there and in Virginia. Once boxed heavyweight champion Jack Dempsey. Worked for Tom Dewey in the war crimes trials. A lawyer. An entrepreneur. Founder of several state and national associations. Husband to the beautiful and charming Trudy. Father. Mentor to thousands. Cavett Robert was all this and much more.

Cavett was, for me, a "dream merchant." He believed so in his dreams that he made me believe in his dreams. And he helped me to believe in my own. Somehow, his vision was wide enough and broad enough to include many ideas and many people. Cavett always seemed to be on fire. He set many others of us to flame as well. While igniting his sales or management audiences, he was also igniting a new industry.

I knew Cavett for nearly 30 years. He was probably the most unselfish man I have ever met. His focus was always on others. There are countless stories to support this.

My very first encounter with this man — who did not become a professional speaker until after his 60th birthday! — was in my hometown, Charlotte, North Carolina. It must have been the late '60s. I had a TV talk show, and Cavett had accepted my invitation to be a guest on it. I also was a wanna-be speaker and wanted to meet this man. Cavett had come to town to speak to the Sales and Marketing Executives dinner meeting. He also did a two-hour afternoon seminar. This Mississippi man, who lived in Phoenix by this time, was all energy, fun, wisdom and positive thinking. His passion was so contagious.

We did the TV show at noon, then had lunch. I was in awe. Cavett talked of his dreams for a speakers' organization. His enthusiasm was contagious. He named 25 or more men and women who might benefit. We could all ante up a little (turned out to be 50 bucks) and create this synergistic organization. "We won't be competing," he assured us, "we'll just be creating a bigger pie!"

Cavett was so convincing. His dreams became mine. And think of it . . . I was on a first-name basis with this giant! He made me feel so special. Planting seeds everywhere he went, he fanned them with passion. And they were taking root!

Little did I know how much this giant could accomplish using the very tools he spoke of at that afternoon and evening's presentations. Nor did I realize how much work it would be to form a national speakers' association. Of course, Cavett and Merlyn Cundiff did all the work and paid for most of it. Vision and hard work paid off. Cavett's dream came true.

The National Speakers Association became a reality for three dozen or so of us in 1973, and the rest is NSA history. Cavett's passion and dreams will live on in all of us and our successors for generations. Who knows what marvelous ultimate conclusion there will be to this dream?

So, Cavett Robert was many things to many of us who profit from his vision. This dream merchant sold his audiences on his inspiration and wisdom. He also created a home for thousands of new speakers as he defined a new profession.

I shall always treasure having known Cavett and Trudy. They truly changed my world!

—TY BOYD

CAVETT'S MISSION TO 'BUILD A BIGGER PIE'

As I walked through the doorway, along with 1,000 others, to take my seat for the upcoming seminar, there stood our speaker. He hadn't been introduced yet and could certainly have stayed backstage to prepare. But here he was, shaking hands and passing out smiles to every person who entered.

The man was Cavett Robert. The year was 1977. The place, Tulsa, Oklahoma. That greeting became a metaphor for Cavett's leadership of NSA. During the 20 years between then and now, he was always greeting people, passing out smiles and praising the best in others. He arrived early and sat in the front row for everything . . . not to get the best seat, but to give the best support. If Cavett was in your audience, your speech was going to be its best.

I recall Cavett sitting in the front row even when I was leading orientations for newcomers to our conventions. He attended small showcase presentations and large events alike. And he always found something encouraging to say to the speakers . . . nobody could give out praise like Cavett. He wrote notes, left messages, gave hugs and found the part of you that most needed love at that moment. He also refused, silently, to participate in any conversation that criticized or ran down another person. The man had dignity. His capacity for affirming people was amazing.

I recall Cavett's comments at a casual lunch we shared last summer. He said, "You guys have done so much more with this (NSA) than I ever imagined possible." He was the one who inspired us to build NSA, yet he gave us the credit for it. One of his favorite quotes was, "It's amazing how much people can do when they divorce themselves from concern over who gets the credit." (I think he was quoting Dr. Peale on that one.)

Cavett belonged to a study group known as the Speakers Roundtable (formerly Speakers Associates). This group of 20 top speakers and trainers meets each summer for four days to help each other grow and enjoy good social times with their families. In the winter, we hold skill-building sessions with professional speech and acting coaches. Cavett attended the group's activities well into his 80s — not just as an audience member, but up on the speaking platform — practicing his material and getting pointers from the coaches. What an inspiration! Long after building his industry association and molding the entire speaking profession, he was still working on his craft, claiming, "School is never out for the pro!"

When I joined NSA in 1976, it was simply a club of 200 or so people who made all or most of their living by giving speeches. It was definitely not a "profession." But in Cavett's mind it was, and through his persistent encouragement, it became one. In NSA's first years, Cavett spoke at almost every meeting. He always said, "It's time we stopped fighting over the size of our piece of the pie and started working together to build a bigger pie." And that's exactly what happened.

Today, there is more opportunity for a person wanting to speak for a living than ever before. The speakers group became a club. The club became an association. The association spawned a profession. All because of Cavett Robert.

It is said that if you want to live a long and fruitful life, find something bigger than yourself to work on. Always have something to look forward to. Cavett Robert lived that advice. His life was abundant beyond the largest dreams of most of us.

The world is a better place because Cavett Robert lived in it. His influence will affect many generations. He has truly blessed us. May God continually bless Cavett Robert.

—JIM CATHCART

THREE MEMORIES OF CAVETT

1. I met Cavett in May of 1968 in San Francisco. I was the manager of a company called American Salesmasters. We were the first company in America to put on for-profit public rallies/seminars featuring top professional speakers. Among the original founders of the company were Zig Ziglar, Hal Krause and Thom Norman.

   Cavett had been contracted to speak on programs throughout the United States and Canada. On this particular one (where we had more than 2,000 in attendance, with no advertising; we did it making "cold call" sales presentations to businesses), the speakers were Cavett, Bob Richards, Kenneth McFarland, Dr. Maxwell Maltz and Fred Herman. Cavett was the least well known of the speakers yet was dynamic and incredibly well received.

   About a year later, American Salesmasters became the first company in the world to start marketing audio cassette tapes of live-recorded speeches of professional speakers. Cavett was one of the speakers on the first set of tapes. In late 1969, we had a meeting in Mexico City at which several American Salesmasters management people got together to present a package to a major company's international sales meeting. As part of the program, Cavett was to be the speaker provided by American Salesmasters. I enjoyed sharing time with him and truly getting to know him in Mexico. Never has there been a more delightful gentleman, and I'm thankful I got to witness him in action almost 30 years ago, in the most unlikely of locations.

2. I still have a file with probably 30 handwritten notes Cavett sent me over the years. They were always positive, always affirming and always remembered. He was the master of writing personalized notes to people. Many of us talk about how nice an idea it is to write such notes, how customers and friends appreciate it, etc., but Cavett was the first person I knew who really practiced it to the ultimate extent. I'm sure hundreds of other speakers have a file of note cards from him, like I do.

3. When I was NSA president from 1980 to 1981, we went on the first winter-workshop cruise. It was wonderful. Because I was president, my wife and I were invited to sit at the captain's table for dinner on Saturday night. Every time I saw Cavett after that, he always reminded me of how nice it was for me to invite Trudy and him to sit with us at the captain's table. Although I never found out the true story, I had always felt that Cavett was the one asked to sit at the table, and since I was the association's president, he had invited Colleen and me to sit with Trudy and him.

Cavett was one of the finest, gentlest, kindest, most humble people I ever knew. While I am very proud of having received the Cavett Award in 1990, I will never be able to live up to many of his incredibly wonderful, positive traits.

125

—MIKE FRANK

'EXCEPTIONAL GENEROSITY'—THE CAVETT NORM

Cavett always wanted his money's worth out of life! His incredible energy never ceased to amaze me. In 1977, I attended my first NSA convention and was tremendously excited at the prospect of attending Cavett's weekend seminar with Merlyn Cundiff. Cavett had flown in just a few hours earlier and had been up all night. But even with no sleep, he was a magnificent and vibrant speaker.

The last time I saw Cavett was at the Speakers Roundtable meeting in the summer of 1997, after the NSA convention. We were a group of about 32, including spouses. Cavett and Trudy had stayed up late the preceding night for the dinners and events, yet there they were, looking fresh and rested at the 7 a.m. prayer meeting. Nearly half their age, I knew I could never have done it.

Cavett's extraordinary skills made even "old-timers" feel like kids in the business by comparison. His stories were always exhilarating and vivid. When he recounted his conversations with Dr. Norman Vincent Peale, he had the ability to make us feel like we knew Dr. Peale as well as he did.

Cavett was unfailingly generous. In 1981, he flew — at his own expense — to address my Sales and Marketing Executives club in San Francisco. We didn't have enough money to pay him, but that didn't stop him from making it a spectacular event. (While he was there, I became the only NSA past president to cut his hair. We both thought he looked great!)

All of us are constantly meeting speakers from all over the country who were also encouraged by Cavett. At every convention coffee break, you hear stories like this one: Leslie Miller from Washington listened to a tape of Cavett and was so inspired, she picked up the phone to tell him how much he had influenced her. She knew nothing about NSA and had no idea who he was. He invited her to visit if she was ever in the area. She took him up on his offer, and he took her for lunch at his club.

Later, at Cavett's home, Leslie saw photos of Billy Graham and Richard Nixon, and Cavett sheepishly admitted that, well, yes, he had started this organization called NSA. He was so comfortable with the situation that it was impossible for her to be embarrassed. Cavett becomes even more special and inspirational when we realize that this type of exceptional generosity was not an occasional gesture. This was the Cavett norm.

—PATRICIA FRIPP

I REMEMBER CAVETT . . .

Cavett and I shared a friendship with a speaker named Bob Bale, who was both a genius and a card-carrying nutcake.

Bob's early days were spent in the rodeo business. Describing that time, he'd say: "I used to ride a horse into the arena and pick up a handkerchief off the ground with my teeth in front of a packed, cheering grandstand. For an encore, I'd turn the horse around, go under his belly . . . and pick up my teeth!

Bob wrote a book titled (honest) *How to Build an A-bomb in Your Bathtub.* The Secret Service came to visit him (would I lie to you?), saying, "Stop that experiment . . . you're getting too close!"

Once, during a drive from Phoenix to Los Angeles for a two-man sales rally, Bob and I were talking golf. He said he'd just gotten a new driver that enabled him to really "crank 'em out there . . . as far as 300 yards!"

I responded, "Now, Bob . . . you've gone too far. Picking a handkerchief off the ground with your teeth while riding a horse? OK . . . I'll give you that. The A-bomb in the bathtub? I'll cross my fingers and allow that maybe that could have happened. But I know a little bit about golf, and come on . . . 300 yards?? Next thing you'll tell me is that they want you for a space flight . . . ."

"Well," Bob began to reply, "as a matter of fact, NASA did call, and . . . ."

"Hold it, Bob!" I stopped him in midsentence. "Like I said, you've gone too far!"

Well, we were getting close to Los Angeles by that time and decided to pull over at the sign saying Driving Range. I'm sure many of you know the story. That's right . . . Bob drove the ball 300 yards — plus! Like I said — genius, maybe . . . nutcake, for sure.

So, here's the rest of the Bob Bale story — the part that involves Cavett . . . .

Sometime in the mid-'70s, Bob was involved in a horrible head-on car collision. When Cavett called to tell me about it, he choked up and said, "There's nothing left of him, Bill . . . nothing left. It's awful!"

Well, with a lot of help from his wife, Doris, Bob was able to get around with crutches and a hideous-looking back brace. Now, here's where Cavett really came into the picture.

Over the next few years, while Bob was still alive, Cavett accepted speaking dates with a certain stipulation. "Yes, I'd be delighted to meet with your group," he'd say, following his acceptance with a description of Bob's situation and this qualification: "Bob and I work as a team. I accept, but Bob has to be on the platform with me. I'm sure you can find a 15- or 20-minute spot for him. He's a great speaker, and when he tells his story, It Only Hurts When I Laugh, there won't be a dry eye in the house!"

In those days, Cavett was one of the busiest speakers in America . . . but then again, so was Bob Bale!

What a man was Cavett Robert . . . what a man!

—BILL GOVE

THE CONSUMMATE PROFESSIONAL AND PERENNIAL STUDENT

Let me pose a problem. Imagine that your best friend of 25 years has died. You have counted this man as your mentor, your idol, your confidant and your guru. You have hired him to speak with and/or for you at least 200 times. You have not only worked together, but his wife and you and your spouse take vacations together and are great friends. You have been asked to pay homage to him in less than 750 words. The problem: how to condense your knowledge of this great man into a meaningful tribute.

Cavett was the consummate professional at everything he did, ranging from being the Arizona Men's Amateur Golf champion to being the Toastmasters International Speech champion. In spite of his fame and high visibility, he was never too busy to be immersed in his own self-improvement. It was common to see him traveling from city to city with a small bag containing 20 to 30 loose audio cassettes and his ever-present tape recorder.

On two different cruises we took together, he showed up with his trusty bag. When I asked why he would carry this stuff on a vacation, he told me that we were to be gone two weeks and he needed to stay abreast of his speaking skills. I later learned that the tapes were of him doing keynotes and seminars. Here was a man at the top of his career who was listening to "self-improvement tapes" — not others', but his own! He was practicing his own belief that "School is never out for the pro."

Cavett would go out of his way to hear anyone speak. Many times, he would be the only high-visibility speaker a client would hire for a given program. He would either open or close a convention, or a day's activity, with a speech. Whenever possible, he would plan to arrive early or stay after his talk to hear other speakers. He would always be sitting in the front row, encouraging them and praising them afterward.

Cavett's hero was the late Will Rogers. Will was noted to have said that he'd never met a man he didn't like. Those of us who knew him well used to kid Cavett by telling him that he'd never met a speaker he didn't like. Cavett spent his life encouraging would-be speakers, sometimes to a fault. Until his dying day, he always had time for anyone seeking his advice.

Here's an example of Cavett's professionalism that I witnessed firsthand. I had hired Cavett for the closing spot at a multi-speaker rally in Sacramento. He flew in around noon with a horrible cold — a fever and a voice nearly gone due to a sore throat. I tried to get him to bed, since he wasn't scheduled to speak until 9 that night. He wouldn't hear of it, though, and disappeared into the crowd. As the program's emcee, I had the occasional need to go from one side of the stage to the other. During one such crossing, I nearly tripped over Cavett! Bundled up in the grand piano cover, he was sitting on the floor, listening to the other speakers. When I introduced him that night, not a soul in the audience could tell he'd been sick a day in his life!

Without question, Cavett's greatest professional accomplishment involved his work in forming this speakers' association. As a lawyer, Cavett was well aware that most professions had an association to serve their members . . . attorneys had the American Bar Association, doctors had the American Medical Association and so on. Sadly, there was no organization to represent the profession of speaking. Cavett dwelled on the idea to start a speakers' association for so long that he no longer had the idea . . . the idea had him!

With the help of his partner at the time, Merlyn Cundiff, Cavett laid out his plans to realize his dream. He enlisted a handful of his closest speaker friends, and they began to spread the word about the new, nameless association that was to become the National Speakers Association. The journey wasn't an easy one. Cavett poured his life and a ton of money into this effort. He promised that he would never become an officer or take a management role in NSA. It took two years of hard work to get 60 people together for their first convention in 1973.

I remember Cavett contacting his friend, Dr. Norman Vincent Peale, about joining the association. Dr. Peale told him that, as positive a thinker as he was, he wouldn't join until the association had made it one year. One year later, Cavett called, and Dr. Peale sent in his check. As this is written, Cavett's dream has materialized and evolved over 25 years, and its 4,000 members are a monument to this great man's vision. God bless you, Cavett.

—D. JOHN HAMMOND

DON'T THROW A SECOND ROUND OF 'SNOWBALLS'!

My favorite Cavett story involves the frantic pace and hectic scheduling that was Cavett's practice for many years. It was not unusual for Cavett to do 200 to 250 presentations each year. He would often arrive shortly before he was scheduled to go on and dash out the door within minutes after he finished.

Cavett had a talk he called, "You Can't Heat an Oven With Snowballs." He gave the talk hundreds of times all over America. Clearly, "Snowballs" was his talk.

In one instance, Cavett arrived at a speech location minutes before he was to be introduced. With no time to visit, he announced to the meeting planner, "Introduce me, coach . . . I'm ready to go on." The meeting planner, vastly relieved that the great Cavett Robert had shown up, strode briskly to the microphone and made the introduction.

Cavett hit the platform in full strut. He was a tornado on stage. He moved with the grace of a panther. His gestures were like lightning bolts. There was enormous power in his voice, great eloquence in his words and tenderness in his heart. He gave what some would say was his best deliverance of "Snowballs."

Cavett later said that audience not only sat there in embarrassed silence, but some members seemed openly hostile. At the finish, where he usually welcomed a raucous standing ovation, there were only scattered claps throughout the room.

Cavett was stunned. He staggered off the stage to confront the wide-eyed, barely audible meeting planner, who stammered, "Mr. Robert, this morning's keynote speaker gave that same talk . . . word for word." It turns out that the keynote speaker had memorized Cavett's tape and made "Snowballs" his own!

Lesson learned: If at all possible, hear the speakers who precede you, or at least check them out. You never know when your signature story will be appropriated by another speaker. If a speaker tells your story first, you will be blamed for using his or her material.

—ROBERT H. HENRY

THE GREATEST ENCOURAGER WHO EVER LIVED

I have so many wonderful memories of Cavett Robert that I don't know where to start in this recap of our 30-year friendship.

This man was incredible. Among the most notable of his qualities was the genuineness of his friendship — no pretense, never a hidden agenda, always selfless and, of course, he always brought bright rays of sunshine with him into any room. His optimism was contagious, even to the extent of encouraging young would-be speakers to "go for it" when their talent was unapparent — sometimes bordering on nonexistent. Cavett was the greatest encourager who ever lived, and I was certainly a beneficiary of this trait.

In the late 1970s, I was asked to speak at the Cavett Robert Tribute and Roast. I really don't remember my remarks that night, but I vividly recall a skit several of his friends staged. In it, the Cavett character went to a diner, where he was waited on by an unsophisticated, gum-smacking waitress whom the Cavett character proceeded to convince to forget waitressing immediately and become a professional speaker! It was hilarious . . . we were practically falling out of our chairs laughing, including Cavett.

From Cavett, I learned:

It is impossible to outgive yourself.

It really is OK to dry your underwear on a hotel-room lamp if you are well practiced in the art.

"Stick to your knitting" — figure out what you do well, and then turn on the after-burner doing it.

Don't ever compromise your integrity, and if you err, do it on the side of generosity.

Cavett lived an incredible life. With movie-star handsomeness and Southern gentility, he did everything he ever attempted well. He was a scratch golfer and used to play in lots of clients' convention tournaments with fellow speaker Bob Bale. Cavett and Bob's popularity on the golf course was not nearly as great as on the platform, since they usually won the tournaments. Cavett also was an accomplished Bonanza pilot, with lots of great stories to amuse us aviators.

Our NSA founder and the namesake of the association's Cavett Award came to me after one of our first board meetings and said he had a plan. Bill Gove, already a speaking legend and admired by all, should be the first NSA president. The highly esteemed and eloquent Dr. Carl Winters had agreed to be NSA's second president. Cavett felt that I, in my relative youth — 29 at the time — would make an energetic and inspirational third NSA president. There were, in truth, many people more deserving than I, and it was quite suspect as to whether I had earned the right to serve in that capacity. But you don't say no to Cavett. I worked for NSA and for him, but nobody worked as tirelessly for NSA as Cavett did.

One of my fondest memories of Cavett took place during the last two summers of his life, when, during the Speakers Roundtable meetings following the NSA convention, I (as well as some others) had the pleasure of pushing Cavett's wheelchair for hours through the Edison Exhibit in Fort Myers and The Pageant of the Masters in Orange County. It is probably rather selfish to even mention that, but it felt so good to finally be able to do something for this treasured friend and great man that he couldn't do for himself.

Undoubtedly his finest lifetime move was marrying Trudy, a South Carolina beauty whose charm overshadowed even Cavett's gentility. I'll always remember the first Mother's Day after my mother passed away. Janet and I were in Scottsdale, and Trudy let me "adopt" her for the day. We took her and Cavett to the Camelback Inn for a wonderful Mother's Day celebration.

Cavett, when you read this from your great lectern in the sky, please remember that, among my special and memorable friends, I will always rank you "foist"!

131

—DON HUTSON

EULOGIZING CAVETT — AND THEN SOME

Following are the eulogy, poem and prayer read by Joe Larson at Cavett's funeral service and the NSA memorial service.

Someone recently said, "The world is 1% good, 1% bad and 98% neutral, and that's why what individuals do is so important" . . . individuals like Cavett Robert, whom we honor here today.

A famous man was once asked the secret of his success, and he replied, "You can sum it all up in three little words, and they are: *and then some.* He said that the top people do what is expected of them — *and then some.*

Cavett Robert did just that. In his life's work, he was tops. A man with character, a man with dignity, a man with self-respect and spirit — *and then some.*

Cavett was a tall, rugged man, and when he came out West, you might say he stood tall in the saddle — sort of in the John Wayne style — and he was his own man.

Oh, Cavett loved to tell stories. He wanted and enjoyed other people's company. He was an outstanding listener . . . always proud of other people's accomplishments. He had faith in their ability and was most of all loved for his beautiful messages.

Cavett was a good husband, a good father, a GREAT grandfather, a good son, a good brother — *and then some.*

We are mighty thankful for people like Cavett Robert. He qualified my friends — *and then some.*

Cavett had a passion about speaking. He inspired people with a passion. He spoke with a passion. It showed — *and then some.*

One of the most endearing aspects about Cavett was the way he inspired other people to do their best and to become speakers. In fact, he's responsible for most of the members of the National Speakers Association. Thousands of people chose to become speakers just because Cavett told them they could. It didn't matter what their job was at the time . . . he would tell anyone and everyone that they could become a speaker.

He told this to waitresses, bellhops, flight attendants, the shoe-shine man, maids cleaning his hotel room . . . even desk clerks, gas station attendants, the UPS man and the postman. It didn't matter if it was the kid delivering the newspaper, a hairdresser, the meter reader or even the ice cream man.

It made absolutely no difference what a person did to make a living, from a pharmacist in Alabama to a home economist from Tennessee to a brush maker from Wisconsin to an NFL referee from Carmel. Maybe even some of you . . . maybe he's the reason you became a speaker.

We all owe a great debt to Cavett's inspiration, for without it, many of us would not be where we are today!

I can hear Cavett now. We were in a Chicago cab to O'Hare, and he was on a roll to the driver, who was spellbound — totally amazed that he was destined to be a speaker. At that point, a big tip was his major ambition. Right in his ear, the driver got this message: "You've got to get a glory in the work you do — a hallelujah chorus in the heart of you. You can paint or tell a story, sing or shovel coal — but you've got to get a glory, or your work lacks soul."

Oh, I am positive, as we worship his memory here today, that Cavett is already busy organizing and signing up a flock of angels into a new local chapter of NSA.

A long time ago, a friend gave me a poem she found stuck in a drawer after her mother passed away, and she is positive her mother wrote it. I would like to share it with you. Trudy and family, and each and every one of you, this is what Cavett might very well say to us today.

WHEN I MUST LEAVE YOU

When I must leave you for a little while,

Please do not grieve and shed wild tears,

And hug your sorrow to you through the years.

But start out bravely with a gallant smile,

And for my sake and in my name,

Live on and do all things the same.

Feed not your loneliness on empty days,

But fill each waking hour in useful ways.

Reach out your hand in comfort and in cheer,

And I, in turn, will comfort you and hold you near.

And never, never be too afraid to die,

For I am waiting for you in the sky.

Let us pray:

Lord, Our Father, here we are once again joined together in your name to give thanks and praise for the Cavett we remember.

Thank you, Cavett, for your worth and your love and trust while you were here on earth with us.

Help us to remember you as we look forward to the future, and give us the strength to claim it.

God gave us the insight to be born to live, and we thank you for being an example of the good life we should all be living.

What you were born with was God's gift to you . . . what you have become is your gift to Him.

May we always remember you as an example of what He wanted us to be. Help us to fulfill your wish with a smile and the courage to enjoy so that we may touch the lives of others by bringing peace and joy and happiness as you have done to us forever more.

Amen.

—JOE LARSON

CAVETT'S WORDS KNOW NO END

For my 54th birthday, my eldest son Kevin bought me a Cavett Robert tape album and one of Cavett's books at a used book-store. They were copyrighted 1979. I was thrilled! I didn't realize they were still out there in circulation; in fact, I didn't even know they existed. Wouldn't you like to have your product still being used after almost 20 years?

I then got the bright idea to take the book and album to the 1997 National Speakers Association convention in Anaheim to have Cavett autograph them. When I showed them to him, he was thrilled that I had them and that they were still around after all these years.

Now these two mementos of Cavett's life are in our living room. In the book, he scrawled, in barely legible handwriting, "To Mike, who has given a new pleasure to NSA." In the tape album, he had jotted, "To Mike, he helped us all."

Now, Cavett probably wrote those phrases to many, many people, but they are especially meaningful to me. And if you look a bit deeper, you notice that they represent the unequaled legacy of what Cavett so generously gave to NSA and the speaking profession. No one has given more pleasure or help to our organization or industry than Cavett.

—MICHAEL MCKINLEY

LOVE, INSPIRATION, GREATNESS — CAVETT'S LEGACIES

To have loved and been loved by Cavett Robert has been one of the highlights of my life. He, more than any other individual, has inspired me to devote a major part of my professional life to the development of professionals in the speaking industry and to the strengthening of our beloved National Speakers Association.

The proudest moment of my career occurred in 1994, when Cavett presented me with the award named after him. I shall always treasure my memories of him and am reminded of them daily as I look upon the image of one of the greatest men I have ever known.

—GEORGE MORRISEY

135

THE MASTER BAKER

Cavett Robert always spoke about "making the pie bigger." If ever there was a baker who put together quality ingredients to end up with a product that was even more than what the recipe originally called for, it was this unforgettable man.

Cavett Robert. The first time I heard that name, I thought how unusual it was, and to this day, I have never heard of anyone with that first name. How fitting that he would have a name like no other, because he was a man like no other.

Can you imagine my surprise and delight, after attending my first NSA convention in New Orleans in 1980, to receive a cassette tape from a man whose name had been mentioned over and over at the convention? I must admit, I was so new to the association, I was not really sure who he was or what he had done. All I knew was that this man with the unusual name was sending me an audiotape, and I wondered what it was all about.

As I played the tape, I heard Cavett's voice saying, "Rosita . . . you precious, precious lady! Ah am sending you this tape from Denvah, Colorado, where ah am about to speak with sales and mahketing executives. Ah was thinkin' about you aftah we left New Ahlins and wanted to contact you to encourage you and to tell you how special ah think you ah."

(Many years later, I found out that every human being who crossed the path of Cavett's life was special to him. But that fact has never diminished the value of what he said to me.)

"You have a very special talent, and ah want to congratulate you and tell you how much ah enjoyed your music and your talk in New Ahlins," the tape's message continued.

It is now 18 years later, and I still remember that tape and that moment and the feeling I had as I listened to this man's voice telling me what I most needed to hear. In the ensuing years, I have concluded that the speaking profession is a lonely one. Although we do our thing in front of thousands of people, when we are finished, we end up in a hotel room alone, wondering if what we did will have an impact on our audience members' lives. Because after the emotion of a standing ovation subsides, after the hugs and kind comments are over, most of us are very interested in knowing that what we do really matters long after we speak.

By reaching out to a newcomer and taking the time to send not just a note but an audiotape filled with encouragement and kind words, Cavett Robert gave me a gift that has kept on giving. Because he was so helpful to me, I decided that I would someday do the very same thing for other NSA newcomers. It fills me with happiness to know that is exactly what I did. Years later, as people thank me for reaching out to them, I smile, knowing that my teacher was Cavett Robert.

The story I have just related could probably have been written by a thousand other people, because that is simply the kind of human being Cavett was. He made a difference. In all the years I knew him, never once did I hear a negative thought or expression come from him. He would sit in the front row, being a cheerleader to newcomers who were doing a 12-minute showcase, many of whom would say afterward, "I can't believe Cavett Robert would come to this session!"

I am so thrilled that Cavett Robert came to our session. "Our session" is this life we're living, and I am richer because of him.

—ROSITA PEREZ

THE SPIRIT OF CAVETT

I've been a professional speaker since 1969, but I never heard Cavett Robert deliver one of his speeches. I was busy with my own career and did not join NSA until 1986. By that time, Cavett's speeches were a rarity. Publishing this book was not important to me because of Cavett, the speaker. It became important to me because of Cavett, the man.

Four of my children went with me to the NSA Palm Springs convention. We connected through Phoenix, and Cavett and Trudy were on the same flight. As we waited, I introduced Cavett to my children. He spent the next 20 minutes asking them about their interests, hobbies and ambitions — and said little about himself. I don't think Cavett knew much about me. I certainly wasn't important in NSA. Cavett talked with my children because he was genuinely interested in them. That made a deep and lasting impression on me.

The last several years of his life, each time I went to Phoenix, I'd get together with Lee, Cavett and Trudy. What an opportunity to listen and learn — but more than that, to absorb his spirit! What I quickly learned is that you had to pay real attention to keeping the conversation focused on Cavett. If you didn't, he quickly returned the conversation to you.

The last several Christmas seasons, we'd have brunch together at the Biltmore in Phoenix. One time Cavett said to me, "You know, if I had it to do all over again, I'd spend less time speaking and more time training. You have a bigger impact on people when you spend more time with them." It meant a lot to have what I do most (which is training) validated by Cavett.

And that was (and is) the spirit of Cavett. He validated people, encouraged them, gently did everything he could to help them bring out the best in themselves.

That's why this book is important. To help people who may never have had a chance to meet Cavett understand who he was and what he represented. It is a spirit that has made NSA a place where people can share, grow and nurture each other. It is a spirit that we need to cherish and keep alive through our own words and actions.

Cavett did indeed leave a lasting legacy. It is not one left through his children alone. It is a legacy left through the organization he founded, the National Speakers Association, and through the leaders and members of the association as we continue to let the "spirit of Cavett" guide the decisions that we make in the years ahead.

It is my prayer that this book will help us all continue to learn from Cavett, his life and his spirit.

—BOB PIKE

HIS SPIRIT AND IMPACT WILL LIVE ON

If it weren't for Cavett, I would not have been a member of NSA. It was his constant prodding in the early 1970s that made me join the organization and his insistence that I keynote his Phoenix Summer Sales Seminar that brought me to the first NSA convention.

Cavett and I met in Atlanta when we both addressed a national trade association convention. He was the legendary dean of the platform, and I was the hopeful novice. No sooner had I finished speaking than he began complimenting me and assuring me that my career in this business would be extraordinary. His exaggeration was music to my ears, and his encouragement was most helpful.

Over the years, Cavett and I developed a wonderful friendship. His guidance and advice were always useful and appreciated. Along with Jim Tunney and me, Cavett signed the first document establishing the National Speakers Association Foundation, which has helped so many over the years and which today enjoys a significant endowment. Cavett was always at the cutting edge of whatever is meaningful for the common good — and NSA was at the top of that list.

The spirit of Cavett Robert will live forever. The impact of his work will permeate all that we do for generations to come.

—NIDO R. QUBEIN

FRONT ROW CENTER

I remember when

I first met Cavett Robert;

I remember when

I last was with Cavett Robert . . .

and the hundreds and hundreds of times in between.

I know that every person who knew and loved Cavett Robert can share a story similar to mine. He became, for all of us, a "front row center" person, in the "balcony of our lives" . . . cheering us on to our highest and our best!

Cavett was the ultimate empowerer of others. He could have been the author of the primo book on empowerment, such was his total belief, encouragement, ability to project power and love into your trembling heart to propel you on to accomplishment and mission.

There are few people in one's life who hold this precious place, few who can make you feel like you are the only one, the best one, the most awesome one for the job, the platform, the challenge. And yet, you knew deep down that Cavett made every person he met feel exactly the same way!

My professional friendship with Cavett started in June of 1977 at my first NSA convention, held at the Biltmore Hotel in Phoenix.

A keynoter for that convention but not yet an NSA member, I was unaware of the synergy that had already become a moving, vital force in the future of professional speaking: the National Speakers Association. This association, founded by Cavett to expand the breadth of the platform, became so much more as he infused his philosophy of sharing, helping, encouraging and celebrating the growth of other professionals as you yourself grew.

On that first meeting day, I was the recipient of Cavett's philosophy, love and concern as I poured out my message and heart in a speech titled "A Very Special Gift." I certainly was not aware that the most special gift was about to be returned to me. Of course, Cavett said I was "the best he had heard," that my speech was "unforgettable" . . . and he continued to remind me of that for the next 21 years.

I was soon privileged to serve on the NSA board of directors, with Cavett always front row center as the organization's founder and chairman emeritus. There, I saw his careful guidance of our association's purposes and future and regularly experienced his empowerment of me personally as a maturing NSA leader.

I had several opportunities to seriously consider running for the presidency of our association — opportunities I consistently rebuffed, refuting the call and doubting my abilities. Finally, in a truly emotional moment, Cavett got down on his knees and, with tears in his eyes, said, "I am praying that God will let me live long enough to see you become president of the National Speakers Association. You just must do it, for us all." And I did! I said yes. How could anyone resist such love and belief?

Through my tenure up the NSA "ladder" of offices, and during my final year as the organization's president in 1993-94, there was no one more encouraging to me than Cavett. Literally and figuratively, he was always front row center, leading the applause.

At one point during my leadership, I presented footballs imprinted with the logo and theme for the year— "The Privilege of the Platform" — to all board members and, of course, to Cavett. We all signed them, and, in classic "Cavett style," he emotionally accepted the football and said, "This means so much to me that I want to be buried with it."

I also was privileged to be part of the Speakers Roundtable with Cavett and to benefit from his indomitable spirit and wisdom right up until the last few weeks of his life. Facing the possibility of Cavett's death was very difficult for me. Just two months after I had been privileged to receive the Cavett Award at the NSA convention in July of 1997 (I was the last recipient to be presented the award by Cavett himself), Cavett's life seemed to be threatened.

And yes, I remember the last time I saw Cavett. It was during a hospital visit. There was praise, once more, for our championing of "his club," there was love and applause for who we were to him and there was "the platform" as we stood around his bed, saying goodbye and singing "Amazing Grace" together.

A few days later, speaking in Toronto, we got the news of his death. The shock, the sadness and the denial set in . . . and then, as I got into the elevator to return to my platform, I had an awareness of a balcony of people cheering me on. And yes, there he was — Cavett Robert, front row center! — always wishing me the best, as he does every person, every speaker he ever met. There will probably never be a speech I give in the future not attended by that wonderful balcony presence of Cavett Robert.

The rest of the story? Yes, the football was buried with Cavett, as he wished — a treasure representing, in a finite way, our giving back to this great man, mentor and friend.

What a truly "lasting legacy of love" Cavett continues to leave to me from . . . front row center!

—NAOMI RHODE

140

AN EVENING WITH CAVETT

A number of ideas flickered through my mind when I was asked to submit a Cavett story. For example, in 1978, I flew to Chicago to take Cavett's course on professional speaking. It was a big decision, because I had never heard of Cavett Robert or NSA and had been winging it on my own for years. I was apprehensive about spending the money and giving up the time to go. Although this wonderful experience could make a good story, I've decided not to tell it, because it would not be unique. Hundreds of speakers took Cavett and Merlyn Cundiff's course through the years or heard them at NSA and could share a similar story.

Well, I thought, maybe I could tell a couple of the funny anecdotes from the boocoodles of Cavett/NSA board of directors memories. It was my good fortune to serve on the NSA board when Cavett played an active role as its wise advisor. Those stories could certainly be of interest. But here again, any number of people could share anecdotes from those days.

OK, then, I could modestly share how excited I was when Cavett told me that he thought I had a lot of talent and that I would go "right to the top." But once again, many speakers . . . and flight attendants and cab drivers and waitresses . . . could relate their accounts of receiving that encouragement. Nope, I decided, I won't dwell on that.

Next, I thought that perhaps I could search for words to describe the sick, stabbing pain in my stomach several times when Cavett spoke at NSA in the twilight of his career. More than once, he paused so long I thought he was lost, and I teared up with anxiety as I hoped he could recall where he was in his remarks. Maybe I could find the words to express my extreme relief when he finally did. But I'm a humorist. Sentimental words don't flow as easily as adlibs.

So, after much thought, I decided to share the Cavett memory that means the most to me — the one I cherish above all others. It isn't earth-shattering; heck, it's not even funny. But it is nice . . . just like the man.

Cavett was scheduled to speak at the Carolinas Speakers Association chapter meeting on a Saturday morning in January, 1990, and was scheduled to arrive the day before. I planned to attend the meeting, too, and was asked if I would come to Charlotte early and have dinner with him on Friday night while the board convened. This meant that just Cavett and Jeanne would spend a couple of hours together in the hotel restaurant. No audience. No other speakers. No table of eight. Just Cavett and me. I was thrilled.

This event occurred long after Cavett had founded NSA and gathered every honor bestowed in the speaking profession. It was five years after I had served as NSA president and six months after its namesake had handed me the Cavett Award at NSA, a memory I will always cherish.

Cavett and I had swapped stories on many occasions with other speakers and in small groups, but on this night, it didn't seem necessary to discuss "making it" in the speaking profession or the challenges of a rapidly growing association we both loved. No, on this night, we just sat in the restaurant and talked about Cavett's early years and his family. And yes, he asked about mine also. No jokes or one-liners. No story topping. No trying to impress. We were just two friends, taking time to go past the veneer so prevalent in professional speaking relationships. What was to be an early dinner stretched into hours of quiet conversation.

And now, you must be thinking, comes the best part. The closer? The single most valuable piece of advice I gleaned that night? The tidbit that the great Cavett entrusted me with to share later, through a medium such as this? Well, he didn't say it in so many words, but that evening, what I learned from Cavett was the importance of spending quality, one-on-one time with other speakers. After years of working with Cavett Robert, I truly didn't know him as an individual until that evening.

So, maybe Cavett did send a piece of advice through me. Maybe this memorable evening prodded me to send the reminder that we speakers should guard against trying to impress each other and spend more time getting to know each other. I believe that would please the great Cavett Robert very much.

—JEANNE ROBERTSON

AN UNPARALLELED COMMITMENT TO EXCELLENCE

I first met Cavett in 1969, when I was selling tickets for American Salesmasters, the pioneer of the big motivational rally business. On the day before our rally in Denver, it was my honor to pick Cavett up at the airport and drive him to Boulder for a special presentation to all employees of my largest customer. During the 45-minute drive, I was captivated by this man's presence, and as he talked to me, I was amazed at the magnificent way he expressed his ideas.

I had previously worked at General Electric and had met many impressive people, but never in my life had I met a conversationalist like this man. We arrived in Boulder with hardly a word uttered by me, but I was thrilled by what Cavett had shared and its value to me. I proudly introduced him to my audience, and he had them in the palm of his hand instantly. As I listened to his words, I experienced a growing sense of familiarity with the message . . . déjà vu! Suddenly, I realized that Cavett had been "practicing" his speech on me all the way from the Denver airport!

Today, I realize that part of the big, big legacy Cavett left us was his absolute commitment to excellence and the hours of practice it requires. It wasn't unusual for him to give two or three speeches in separate cities, all on the same day. On the day I drove him from Denver to Boulder, his commitment to excellence drove him to polish some of the key vignettes he would use that day — parts of a speech he probably hadn't given for at least four or five hours!!

A few years later, I returned to Phoenix to start my own business. Within a month, I received a message that Cavett Robert had called me. Immediately, I assumed he needed a ride to the airport! When I returned his call, he said, "I want you to meet Merlyn Cundiff, because the three of us are going to put on some seminars here in Phoenix this summer." I thought, "Oh, good . . . a little extra money I can make selling tickets." But then Cavett said, "You're going to be one of the speakers." I said, "Cavett, I can talk, but I talk to sell tickets." He said, "Don, I've heard you speak, and you are ready to be a featured speaker."

When the brochure for the first Phoenix Summer Sales Seminar was printed, I thought I would have a little picture down in the corner of the flyer, but I received equal billing with the man with the smallest ego and biggest heart in the speaking profession. Cavett created a self-fulfilling prophecy that hundreds of us, with his love and support, rose to fulfill.

A few years later, Cavett booked a speech and convinced the meeting planner to invite me and one of Cavett's other mentees — my good friend from my ticket sales days, Donny Hutson — to be the other two speakers. I, of course, knew why I was selected — Cavett had told me I was the best young speaker in America. It wasn't until later that I found out he had told Donny the same thing . . . and Donny was wondering why *I* was there.

As Donny and I were standing in the back of the room listening to Cavett and feeling so grateful for his encouragement and for sharing his platform with us, a funny thought came into my mind, and I jabbed Donny in the ribs to share it with him. He said, "What? . . . what??" I said, "Donny, Cavett is really irritating me." In disbelief, he asked, "What's he doing?" I said, "Donny, he's using a lot of our material!" Cavett held back nothing in his desire to help others share in the joy of speaking, and that included "borrowing" material while we were developing our own.

Long before Cavett officially founded the National Speakers Association, he shared an analogy with me that I believe explains part of his motivation to launch NSA. He said, "You know, Don . . . speakers are a lot like truck drivers. They're alone an awful lot. They travel long distances to deliver their payload. While I'm sure most truck drivers appreciate their employers and the customers who make it possible for them to make a living, I believe they feel the closest kinship with other truck drivers. As truckers cruise across the highways of North America, they acknowledge each other with special waves, horns and flashing lights in the night. The truck stop isn't just a place to get food and fuel. For truckers, it's a place to be with that small group of people who truly understand their loneliness . . . and certainly, other truckers share a fierce independence, self-reliance, the monotony of travel and the powerful feeling of controlling a cargo much bigger than they are." He said, "There's a real need to bring that kind of fellowshipping opportunity to combat the loneliness we as speakers can feel as we crisscross our great continent to speak and deliver a message much bigger than we are."

Cavett conceived of NSA, he believed in it, and we are here. I believe our challenge is to continue his legacy.

—DON THOREN

CAVETT'S CODE

I met Cavett Robert in 1976, at the second NSA annual convention. We didn't share much more than a nod and quick "Glad to meet you." Still, I remember the intensity of his aura of energy and kindness. This 60-year-old "beginning" speaker" had the vitality of someone 30 years younger. I was awed.

Three years later, at our fifth convention, in Louisville, I had been nominated for the NSA board of directors. The year was 1979, the first year NSA held elections for the board. (In earlier years, there was a "search" for candidates, and if you said yes, you were "selected.")

The election results were to be announced at the closing luncheon, at which Cavett and I were seated next to each other. I must have shown some nervousness, for Cavett put a hand on my shoulder and said, "You're a cinch to win."

When the results were announced, the sound of my name didn't hit the air. I smile and mumbled, "Well, I'll try again next year." Cavett was shocked that I hadn't made it and said so to everyone within earshot. Then, as he so often did, he took it to the next level. Turning to me, he said, "I'll be sure to help you more next year."

Cavett became one of my closest friends. I always felt a surge of energy in his presence, grateful for the chance to learn from his easy way of offering encouragement and subtle, effective confidence to everyone around him. Possessing an inexhaustibly generous nature, he was a natural mentor to hundreds, more likely thousands, of speakers — NSA members and nonmembers, novices and veterans, both genders, all topics.

I constantly marveled at how naturally Cavett would say everything in the positive. If nerves had a speaker's knees knocking, he would never say anything like, "Stop that shaking." He would bring it around to something bright and powerful, like, "Take a deep breath and let all that great energy flood up to smiling eyes." He never said a negative word about another person. He had the grace of wisdom and the triumph of tolerance guiding every thought and choice.

143

Cavett was a true "lamplighter," and we can show no greater appreciation for him than to stride in his footprints by strengthening our wisdom and giving generously of our time and talents. We can start this minute by beginning to speak only in the positive.

When I won a seat on the NSA board in 1980 and served as president from 1986 to 1987, Cavett enjoyed my accomplishments as much as or more than I did. He always had an open heart, ready to feel good about someone else's effort. He was a genuine humanist, a natural leader, a great friend and a true treasure to everyone who knew him.

—JIM TUNNEY

INSPIRATION THAT MADE OTHERS FEEL '10 FEET TALL AND BULLETPROOF'

What do I remember most about Cavett Robert? His graciousness. A true son of the South, he displayed his genteel upbringing every time I was with him, as did his beautiful wife, Trudy. He constantly reminded me what it looked like to be a gentleman, and Trudy has always been the perfect definition of the word *lady*.

The year I was NSA president, from 1992 to 1993, we had our annual convention in Dallas, Texas, at the Lowe's Anatole. Both Cavett and Trudy were there. I had asked Bill Kneece and his son-in-law, Wade Caughman—both friends of mine in Columbia who were in the video-recording business—to attend the convention and record everything.

After arriving on the scene, I decided I wanted a thorough interview of Cavett and Trudy on video. As happens with so many things in my life, I didn't plan the interview in advance—the reason being, I didn't think of it until after we got to Dallas. So, I asked Cavett if he and Trudy would come to my suite for a couple of hours while we asked questions of the two of them. Judy Kneece, Bill's wife, conducted the interview because I had to be at other meetings.

I joined them near the end of the session and was able to participate a little in the interview. I'll never forget Cavett's response. But before I tell you what it was, I need to tell you how Cavett always responded to everyone. He had the uncanny ability to tune into a person and make him or her feel like the only person in the room and the most important person in the world. I myself had "chased Cavett down" on many previous occasions just to spend a few minutes with him, knowing that when I walked away, I'd feel 10 feet tall and bulletproof.

144

You've probably figured out that Cavett didn't merely say yes to my interview request . . . he made me feel like it was the best idea anyone in NSA had ever had. He came to my suite and spent almost three hours talking about everything under the sun pertaining to NSA: how it got started, what the first meetings were like, how it had grown and where he saw it going.

I treasure the videotape I have of that interview in Dallas. The dignity and grace of Cavett the gentleman was matched only by his passion for NSA. Anytime my enthusiasm wanes for our association, all I have to do is turn on my VCR and TV, plug in that tape, sit back and let Cavett reinspire me to continue the work he started.

—AL WALKER

A SPECIAL THANK-YOU TO ALL FINANCIAL CONTRIBUTORS TO THIS BOOK

Michael A. Aun, Kay Baker, Patricia and Ken Ball, Bill and Sheila Bethel, Lenora Billings-Harris, Joe Bonura, Ty Boyd, William T. Brooks, Joe Calloway, Jack Canfield, Arnold "Nick" Carter, Jim Cathcart, Alan Cimberg, Gerald L. Coffee, Elizabeth Craig, Creative Solutions, John Patrick Dolan, Mike Frank, Scott Friedman, Cathy Fyoch, William H. Gove, T. Scott and Melanie J. Gross, Betty Hardy, Keith Harrell, James F. Hennig, Robert H. Henry, Liz Curtis Higgs, Tom Hopkins, Suzie Humphreys, Janie Jasin, Elizabeth Jeffries, Bill Johnson, Dewitt Jones, Danielle Kennedy, David S. Knox, Janet Lapp, Joe Larson, Karen Lawson, Harvey Mackay, Dennis and Wendy Mannering, Mary Jane Mapes, Suzie H. Mayo, Dennis and Nikki McCuistion, Eileen McDargh, Nancy and Michael McKinley, Jim Meisenheimer, Linda L. Miles, W. Mitchell, George L. Morrisey, Bob Murphey, Patrick O'Dooley, Terry Paulson, Ray Pelletier, Rosita Perez, Bob Pike, Sue Pistone, Connie Podesta, Nido Qubein, Jim and Naomi Rhode, Rita Risser, Jeanne S. Robertson, Mark Sanborn, Speaker for All Persons, Don Thoren, Jim Tunney, Stephen Tweed, Phillip and Susan Van Hooser, Al Walker, Joanne Wallace, Alan Weiss, Larry Winget, Zig and Jean Ziglar.

We also thank those who kindly contributed after this book went to press.

NSA CONVENTIONS

DATE	SITE	ATTENDANCE
1975	Phoenix	not available
1976	Phoenix	not available
1977	Phoenix	not available
1978	Louisville	not available
1979	Scottsdale	not available
1980	New Orleans	not available
1981	St. Louis	700
1982	Chicago	750
1983	San Francisco	800
1984	Phoenix	950
1985	Washington	907
1986	Phoenix	953
1987	Nashville	950
1988	Phoenix	950
1989	Dallas	1000
1990	Atlanta	1000
1991	Palm Desert	1270
1992	Orlando	1150
1993	Dallas	1398
1994	Washington	1582
1995	Minneapolis	1469
1996	Orlando	1925
1997	Anaheim	2011
1998	Philadelphia	2000+ expected

for me, and I hope you [

calendar also. Conditionin

learning and stays with [

well know, we cannot b

and love of each other [

     I've never enjoyed

than my relationship wi

I think I can best expre

Christmas toast:

    "As I lift my glass i

my wealth of many fri

joy, as it does every Ch

hand gently on my shou

to say 'I love you, my pr

     Best of everything

Christmas,